UTILITARIANISM:
A GUIDE FOR THE PERPLEXED

Continuum Guides for the Perplexed

Continuum's Guides for the Perplexed are clear, concise and accessible introductions to thinkers, writers and subjects that students and readers can find especially challenging. Concentrating specifically on what it is that makes the subject difficult to grasp, these books explain and explore key themes and ideas, guiding the reader towards a thorough understanding of demanding material.

Guides for the Perplexed available from Continuum:

UTILITARIANISM:
A GUIDE FOR THE PERPLEXED

KRISTER BYKVIST

continuum

Continuum International Publishing Group

The Tower Building   80 Maiden Lane
11 York Road   Suite 704
London SE1 7NX   New York, NY 10038

www.continuumbooks.com

British Library Cataloguing-in-Publication Data
A catalogue record for this book is available from the British Library.

ISBN: HB: 978-0-8264-9808-3
PB: 978-0-8264-9809-0

Library of Congress Cataloging-in-Publication Data
Bykvist, Krister.
Utilitarianism : a guide for the perplexed / Krister Bykvist.
p. cm.
Includes bibliographical references.
ISBN 978-0-8264-9808-3
ISBN 978-0-8264-9809-0
1. Utilitarianism. I. Title.

B843.B95 2009
171'.5–dc22

2009018064

Typeset by Newgen Imaging Systems Pvt Ltd, Chennai, India
Printed and bound in Great Britain by CPI Antony Rowe,
Chippenham, Wiltshire

For Maya and Vikram

CONTENTS

ACKNOWLEDGEMENTS

I am very grateful to Anandi Hattiangadi and Gustaf Arrhenius who read several drafts of this book and provided extremely useful comments, some of which saved me from silly mistakes and embarrassing philosophical examples. I am also indebted to the undergraduate students in Cambridge and Oxford who were taught portions of the material that later was worked into the book. Their questions and comments helped me present the material in a much more organized and accessible way.

Parts of this book were written during the Fall of 2008 when I was a Fellow at the Swedish Collegium for Advanced Studies (SCAS) in Uppsala, Sweden. I am very grateful to SCAS for their generous financial support and warm hospitality during my stay in Uppsala. The final draft was finished when I was back in Oxford. I am grateful to my college, Jesus College, for granting me the necessary leave to complete the book.

I am also grateful to Geoffrey Ferrari who helped me with the final proofreading of the book manuscript.

Finally, I am grateful for permission to draw upon portions of the following two papers.

Bykvist, K. (2002), 'Sumner on desires and well-being', *Canadian Journal of Philosophy*, Vol. 32, No. 4, (© 2002 Canadian Journal of Philosophy).

Bykvist, K. (2009), 'Preference-formation and intergenerational justice', in Gosseries, A. and Meyer, K., (eds.), *Intergenerational Justice*, Oxford: Oxford University Press (© Oxford University Press), 301–322.

CHAPTER ONE

INTRODUCTION

Utilitarianism states that we ought to make the world as good as we can by making the lives of people as good as we can. On the face of it, this sounds almost trivial. Would anyone claim that we ought to do *less* good than we can and that the world is *not* made better when people are made better off?

Indeed, the sound-bite quality of utilitarianism has always appealed to politicians and economists. Of course, few politicians are card-carrying utilitarians, but they often flirt with utilitarianism in political debates. 'Our party wants to make people better off' is a slogan that is difficult to argue with except that it seems to be stating the obvious. 'This proposal is for the greater good' is more contentious, since it often masks the fact that some people will gain and others lose, but is still offered as a justification that we all can take on board. A more serious commitment to utilitarianism is shown by politicians who believe in a strong welfare state. The rationale for such a state has surely something to do with the importance of promoting the well-being of people. Economists are more open about their utilitarian inclinations when they insist that we cannot make it better for society without making it better for people, and that we cannot make it better for people without satisfying their desires. Moreover, economists often agree with utilitarianism that if we make some people better off and no one worse off, this must be seen as an overall improvement.

Utilitarianism has also played a vital role in the recent animal liberation movement. Indeed, one of the books that inspired this movement was *Animal Liberation* by Peter Singer, a committed utilitarian.[1] What the activists took to heart was the utilitarian concern, first articulated by Bentham, that 'the question is not, Can they *reason*?

nor, Can they *talk*? but, Can they *suffer*?'[2] To downplay the importance of animal suffering is now often seen as a form of speciecism akin to racism and sexism.

Despite its initial attractiveness, it is easy to find faults with utilitarianism, especially when we employ our untutored common sense intuitions. For example, it seems to be *too demanding*, since you may be required to sacrifice your life for the sake of the overall good; *too permissive*, since it will permit you to torture innocent people if that is the only way to avoid serious harm to many others; and *too forgiving of inequalities,* since it does not care about how well-being is distributed between individuals so long as it is maximally promoted.

A version of the last objection, that utilitarianism condones unfair and unequal distributions of well-being, seemed at one point to make it defunct among academic philosophers, especially after John Rawls, in his famous book *A Theory of Justice*, argued that there is a superior alternative.[3] However, recent developments in the utilitarian debate show that the theory is still alive and kicking. Even staunch critics of utilitarianism still define their own positions by contrasting it to utilitarianism. For instance, the critics' papers on ethical issues often have titles beginning with 'A non-utilitarian approach to . . .'.

The main aim of this book is to examine utilitarianism and see whether it can answer the standard objections. However, whenever I consider an objection to utilitarianism I will be careful to point out exactly which aspect of utilitarianism the objection is about. I agree with Fred Feldman that we have a duty to see our theoretical targets clearly before we pull our argumentative triggers.[4] All too often, critics of utilitarianism indulge in a kind of 'Rambo philosophy', criticizing furiously without taking proper aim, with the result that both good and bad aspects of the theory are discarded. My piecemeal criticism will also show exactly *where* utilitarianism goes astray and is in need of revision. It may be possible to make revisions within the limits of utilitarianism, since by refuting one version of utilitarianism we have not automatically refuted utilitarianism *as such*.

It is widely acknowledged that utilitarianism is far from trouble-free, but it is rarely discussed whether other alternative moral theories face similar problems. Another aim of this book is therefore to evaluate utilitarianism, not in isolation, but by comparing it with other theories, in particular, virtue ethics, deontology, and Kantianism. Of course, since this book is a fairly short introduction, I will not be able to go very deep into these alternative theories. But, I think that what I say is enough to show that many of the problems that afflict utilitarianism will also afflict alternative moral theories. In fact, I believe that many of these 'utilitarian problems' are problems for all plausible moral theories. To give a fair assessment of utilitarianism it is therefore crucial to distinguish the problems that are unique to utilitarianism from those that any plausible moral theory will have to grapple with.

To use this comparative methodology successfully, I need to make explicit how we should test a moral theory. In Chapter Two, I will list some fairly uncontroversial constraints on a plausible moral theory. They divide into two kinds: theoretical and practical. Theoretical constraints concern general virtues of theory-building such as simplicity, coherence, explanatory power, as well as more specific virtues of moral theories, such as moral coherence – a plausible moral theory must deliver moral verdicts that, to a large extent, cohere with our firm moral convictions about particular cases. Practical constraints, in contrast, concern the way moral theory is put into action. Can the theory be used by ordinary agents, or does it demand too much of the agent in terms of information, calculation, and motivation?

Most of the discussion in the book will centre on the classical version of utilitarianism, *maximizing act-utilitarianism*, which says that an act is right just in case it leads to more total well-being than any other alternative action. I choose this version for two reasons. First, it is the version of utilitarianism that has received most criticisms. Second, I think that, in the end, it is the best version of utilitarianism. I will give some support for this claim in Chapter Ten where I compare act-utilitarianism with its close relative, rule-utilitarianism, according to which it is the outcomes of rules that determine the rightness of actions, not the outcomes of individual actions.

I want this book to be up to date, so I will spend relatively little time on the classical utilitarians, John Stuart Mill, Henry Sidgwick, and Jeremy Bentham, and instead focus on the most recent developments of utilitarianism. This is not because I think that the predecessors are irrelevant. On the contrary, their pioneering work set the foundations for the various developments to follow. In this book, however, I will not give a separate treatment of their ideas in their historical contexts but try to work their ideas and arguments into the general discussion. I will refer to the old classics only in so far as this helps us define utilitarianism or defend it against its critics. I hope that this will bring them back to life, so that they can be seen more like participants in the current debate rather than dusty items in the museum of thought.

One particularly striking feature of the latest research on utilitarianism is its high level of precision and sophistication. Some of the issues discussed in this book will therefore require some basic knowledge of philosophical ethics. This means that the book is not primarily aimed at beginners in philosophical ethics. However, I will always remind the reader of the basic distinctions and concepts that are important for the issue at hand. I will also provide a list of suggested reading at the end of each chapter, where the reader will find useful background reading as well as more thorough treatments of the issues discussed in the chapter. Even readers who are new to philosophical ethics will therefore benefit from reading the book.

Finally, to be fair to the reader, I think I should put my cards on the table and say something about where I stand in this debate. I am not a convinced utilitarian myself, but I do think that the theory has much more going for it than is usually thought. In the end, I am inclined to think that a non-utilitarian version of consequentialism is preferable, but the utilitarians are surely right that well-being matters a great deal.

The overall outline of the book is as follows.

In Chapter Two I will say something general about what a moral theory is supposed to do. In particular, I shall discuss both its theoretical and practical functions. Once we know what a moral theory is supposed to do we also know how to assess a particular moral theory, such as utilitarianism.

In Chapter Three I shall take utilitarianism apart and identify its basic elements. I shall introduce and clarify one particular form of utilitarianism, maximizing act-utilitarianism, which will be the main target in the critical discussion that follows. Finally, I will give a short introduction to some of the most popular rival moral theories. This will not just deepen our understanding of utilitarianism, since we will know what it rules out, but it will also make it easier to make a comparative assessment of utilitarianism.

Chapter Four deals with the utilitarian conception of well-being. The discussion is focused on the two main candidates for utilitarian well-being: pleasure and desire satisfaction. I will address the standard objections to these candidates, and suggest that by incorporating some objective elements into a desire theory we may get a viable well-being theory that makes well-being morally relevant.

In Chapter Five I shall discuss sum-ranking, the idea that the value of an outcome is equal to the sum of well-being contained in it. I will show that sum-ranking has many controversial implications. For instance, it implies that any loss to one person, no matter how great, can be justified if we make sufficiently many other people slightly better off. Some objectors think that the root of these problems is that the utilitarian treats people as mere containers for well-being and not separate individuals. I will critically examine this suggestion and put forward some utilitarian responses. In particular, I will explore ways sum-ranking could be resisted by a utilitarian.

In the rest of the book, I will focus mainly on the *normative* aspects of utilitarianism, its verdicts about what is right or wrong.

In Chapter Six I will ask whether utilitarianism can function as a guide to action. I will ask whether we can easily *know* what we ought to do according to utilitarianism, and whether we can be *motivated* to follow utilitarianism. I shall also ask whether non-utilitarian moral theories provide more user-friendly guides to action.

In Chapter Seven I shall ask whether utilitarianism is too demanding. For example, is it true that it requires us to perform heroic actions of self-sacrifice for the sake of overall well-being? And how demanding is it compared to alternative non-utilitarian moral theories? I will also discuss the question of whether utilitarians can be true friends.

In Chapter Eight I will discuss the objection that utilitarianism is too permissive. It seems, for instance, to put no moral constraints on our actions. Any kind of action, no matter how intuitively repugnant, will be permissible, indeed obligatory, if it happens to maximize overall well-being. Also, utilitarianism does not give room for any special duties to your own family and friends. For instance, you are permitted, indeed required, to let your own child drown, if you thereby can save two children of a complete stranger. I shall also discuss to what extent a suitably revised form of utilitarianism can accommodate constraints and special duties, and whether in the end it is desirable to accommodate constraints and special duties.

In Chapter Nine I shall consider the objection that utilitarianism does not care about how and why outcomes are brought about, since its only concern is that overall well-being is promoted. I will do this by focusing on one particular case: The Trolley problem.

In Chapter Ten I shall turn to the issue about the proper place for rules in utilitarianism. In particular, I shall discuss rule-utilitarianism, and see whether it is superior to act-utilitarianism.

The final chapter Chapter Eleven, contains a summary of the main points.

CHAPTER TWO

THE NATURE AND ASSESSMENT
OF MORAL THEORIES

In this chapter I will say something in general about the nature of
moral theories such as utilitarianism. In particular, I will state the
primary aims of a moral theory and say something about how to
assess and compare moral theories.

NORMATIVE ETHICS

Consider the following questions:

Was it wrong to invade Iraq?
Can an act of terrorism be right?
Can it be right to clone a human being?
Did we do something wrong last Christmas when we spent so
much money on presents and food for our family and friends
instead of sending it to charities?

These are all pressing normative questions. They are normative in the
sense that they concern the *rightness*, *wrongness* or *obligatoriness* of
actions. Most of us would also think that they are pressing *moral*
questions. For instance, when we ask whether it was wrong for United
States and the United Kingdom to invade Iraq we are not just asking
whether it was rational for them to do this, or whether it served their
interests to do so.

In this book, I will not try to find out what utilitarianism says
about these questions. This might disappoint you. Isn't the primary
aim of a moral theory to answer important moral questions such

as the ones listed above? No, the most central questions for a moral theory are not '*What* is right?' and '*What* is wrong?', but '*Why* is an action right?' and '*Why* is an action wrong?' A moral theory, such as utilitarianism, is thus primarily in the business of finding out what *makes* an action right and what *makes* an action wrong.

Of course, when we have answers to these general questions, we will be in a better position to answer the moral questions about what is right or wrong. Indeed, we will be able to see important connections between different moral questions. For instance, suppose you think that we have a duty to save lives if the costs to us are minor. Suppose you come across a pond where a child is drowning. You could easily save the child by jumping into the pond and pulling her out. The only cost to you is that your fancy new trousers will be ruined. Surely, a life is more important than a pair of trousers! But, then, how could you be justified in not sending money to charities that will save lives in developing countries? The mere fact that they are far away can hardly matter.

To take another example, suppose you think that there is no difference between killing innocent people in order to realize something good, and realizing something good knowing that, as an unintended effect, this will kill innocent people. Then it will be difficult to draw a clear-cut moral distinction between, on the one hand, bombing an ammunition factory in order to stop a war, knowing that this will kill some innocent people living nearby, and, on the other hand, directly killing innocent people in order to cause terror and thereby stop the war.

Finally, suppose you are a driver of runaway trolley with no brakes. You are in a situation where you can either turn left and kill five people standing on the track or turn right and kill one person standing on the track. Surely, you should turn right and kill one person rather than killing five people. But if your reasoning is that it is always right to save as many lives as possible, why shouldn't you kill a healthy patient in order to use her organs to save five other patients who will die if they are not given these organs? (This so-called Trolley problem is the topic of Chapter Nine.)

Of course, knowledge about what makes an action right is not enough to answer particular moral questions. It is still true that in order to answer these questions fully we will need to gather a lot of empirical data as well. For instance, in order to judge whether the invasion of Iraq was wrong we need to know the consequences this will have on Iraqi lives and the political situation in the Middle East.

This short sketch of normative ethics also suggests how it differs from both metaethics and applied ethics. While metaethics is concerned mainly with questions about the nature of moral properties and facts, the meaning of moral terms and utterances, and the knowledge of moral facts (if there are any such facts), normative ethics is concerned with what makes an action right or wrong, not with the nature of the right-making relation or the nature of the rightness property. While applied ethics is mainly concerned with questions about which specific actions are right or wrong, for instance, whether abortion can be justified, normative ethics is more general and provides theories about what makes actions in general, not just abortions, right or wrong.

MORAL THEORY AND THE CRITERION OF RIGHTNESS

It is common in moral philosophy to call the features that explain why an act is right, *right-making features*, and the ones that explain why an action is wrong, *wrong-making features*. So, normative ethics could be seen as a disciplined search for right- and wrong-making features. Now, even if we know that some features are right-making, this in itself does not mean that we know that any act with these features must be right. This might sound paradoxical. But it is easy to explain. Acts can have both right- and wrong-making features. Suppose that you have promised to meet your friend for lunch but on the way to the restaurant you witness a traffic accident. The victim of the accident urgently needs your help. You need to call the ambulance and stay on the scene until it arrives. Unfortunately, if you stay on the scene you will miss your lunch appointment. Should you stay? The fact that you would break a promise is a wrong-making feature of your staying. The fact that you would help the victim is a right-making feature of your staying. In order to decide what is right, *all things considered,* we have to weigh the right-making features against the wrong-making ones. So, when I say that a feature is right-making, I am not saying that any act with this feature is right all things considered; I am saying that the feature counts towards the overall rightness of an action.

It is common to signal that the rightness one is dealing with is not an all things considered rightness by using the term '*prima facie* rightness':

It is prima facie right to keep promises.
It is prima facie wrong to kill a human being.

Sometimes the prima facie claims are expressed in terms of conditionals in which the antecedent explicitly specifies what the right-making features are:

If you have promised to do something, you are prima facie obligated to keep your promise.

Here the fact that you have promised something is assumed to be a right-making feature.[1]

Many moral theories do not just list a set of right and wrong-making features; they also provide a method of weighing these features against each other. Whether this is a bonus is controversial. Those who think it is, often argue that a moral theory cannot be action-guiding if it does not provide a clear method of deciding what is right all things considered. The critics reply that it is a mistake to look for clear methods, or principled ways of weighing right- and wrong-making features. Ethics is not an exact science, they say; instead, we have to rely on intuitions or moral sensibilities that cannot be codified in exact principles.

The theory-friendly camp often goes on to say that any acceptable moral theory can be expressed as a *criterion of rightness*:

An action A is right if and only if A is F.

F-ness is here seen as something that all and only right acts have in common, something that makes all right actions right. F-ness can either be a simple property, or a complex one. Utilitarians, for instance, provide a clear criterion of rightness in terms of a pretty complex property: an act is right if and only if it maximizes total well-being. Some clarifications are important here:

(1) A criterion of rightness is not meant to be a definition of terms. One can accept the criterion of rightness and still deny that

'A is right' means the same as 'A is F'. For instance, even if utilitarians are committed to saying that an action is right if and only if it maximizes well-being, they are not committed to saying that 'x is right' means the same as 'x maximizes overall well-being'.

(2) Nor is a criterion of rightness meant to be a statement of property identity. One can accept the utilitarian criterion of rightness and still deny that the property of being right is the same as the property of maximizing overall well-being. Indeed, it would be odd to accept such an identity claim and also claim that an action is made right by the property of maximizing overall well-being. What makes an action right can hardly be rightness itself. If it did, rightness would explain itself: the fact that the action is right explains the fact that the action is right. But rightness is one thing, what explains it is another.

(3) To talk about a criterion of rightness might suggest a moral litmus test: that 'an action is right if and only if it is F' is a criterion for rightness in the same way as 'something is an acid if and only if it turns the litmus paper red' is a criterion for acidity. But this is a mistake. A litmus test helps us identify acids but does not tell us what makes an acid an acid. In contrast, a criterion of rightness is supposed to tell us what makes an action right.

(4) A criterion of rightness is not the same thing as a decision method or procedure. A criterion of rightness tells you why right actions are right, while a decision method tells you how to decide to act. This distinction is not special to moral theories. You can find it in all goal-directed activities. Basically, it is a distinction between aims and the means to the aims. You might think that the right thing to do is to find a soul mate you can spend the rest of your life with. But if you constantly think about whether the person you are dating is the right one, you might behave awkwardly and scare him away. Constantly thinking about your aim can often be counterproductive. (I will say something more about this distinction in Chapter Six.)

Consequentialists, utilitarians, and Kantians have usually opted for a theoretical approach to normative ethics, aiming at a clear formulation of a criterion of rightness. Virtue ethicists, however, have typically opted for the softer approach according to which there are no precise methods. Now, even if this is a significant disagreement, it is important to remember that all sides accept that normative ethics is about finding right- and wrong-making features. In the following,

I will use 'moral theory' loosely for any moral position that lists some right- or wrong-making features.

HOW TO TEST MORAL THEORIES

In this book, I will assess utilitarianism in part by comparing it to the main contenders in modern normative ethics. But how should we assess moral theories? What are the test questions we should apply when we compare moral theories? They divide into two kinds: theoretical and practical. While theoretical questions concern the theoretical aim of a moral theory, that is, the aim of finding a plausible account of the right- and wrong-making features, practical questions concern how a theory is put into action. More specifically, the test questions can be formulated as follows, starting with the theoretical ones.

(1) Theoretical

(a) Clarity
Is the theory stated in terms of clear and unambiguous concepts? Does the theory have clear implications? It is a sad fact that many ethical theories look attractive at first sight; but when you look closer, you find that they contain so many vague and ambiguous concepts that it is very difficult to say which actions they would prescribe. For example, consider the popular moral claim that it is never right to treat a person merely as a means or the claim that human life is sacred. Do these attractive moral claims allow for killing in self-defence or abortion? There is no telling until the crucial notions 'treating someone merely as a means', 'human life', and 'sacred' have been made more precise.

(b) Simplicity
Is the theory simple? Does it consist of a vast number of complex principles or a few simple ones? All other things being equal, a simpler theory seems to be preferable to a more complicated one. Unnecessary complications should be avoided.

(c) Explanatory power and scope
Does the theory not just entail the right prescriptions but also *explain* *why* these prescriptions are right? Does the theory help us deal with moral questions about which we are not confident, or do not agree?

Does it, for instance, help us to take a stand on the many perplexing problems that arise because of technological advances in medicine?

(d) Internal coherence
Is the theory internally coherent? A logically incoherent theory should be rejected. For instance, a theory that entails that an action is both overall right and overall wrong is hopeless.

(e) Moral coherence
Does the theory have implications that cohere with the moral convictions we have confidence in, after careful reflection? An acceptable theory should match our moral judgements, but not just any old judgements. Some immediate judgements might just be responses distorted by emotional disturbance, self-interest, and social pressure. Your anger and hate may cause you to immediately judge that the criminal who harmed your family should be killed. So we need to see whether our ethical judgements would survive serious reflection in a 'cool hour'. Furthermore, since some considered moral judgements might just be deep-rooted moral prejudices, we need to weed out those judgements in which we would lose confidence once we knew how they were formed. If I was brought up in a community in which I was constantly told, without the backing of any good argument, that people with a certain skin colour are dangerous and ought to be avoided, my considered judgement that I should never mix with these people is a judgement in which I might lose confidence once I knew how it was formed.

There are two questions about moral coherence that need to be singled out. One is the question of whether the theory is too demanding: Does it place demands on us that we intuitively find too stringent? Does it require us to become moral saints, for instance?

The other is the question of whether the theory is too permissive: Does it deem permissible actions that we find clearly impermissible after careful reflection? Does it, for instance, say that it is right to kill a healthy patient in order to use her organs to save five other patients? As we shall see in later chapters, these two questions are particularly pressing for utilitarianism.

(2) Practical

Is it possible to use the theory as a guide to action when you deliberate about what to do?

A moral theory seems useless if it can never guide agents when they deliberate about what to do. This question can be broken down into the following questions:

(a) Does it give prescriptions that we can follow? For example, a theory that sometimes tells you to do A and not to do A cannot guide your actions in all situations.
(b) Does it require too much information or information that is difficult to gather, for instance, information about the distant past, your own subconscious motivations, or the consequences of your actions in the far future?
(c) Does it require too much calculation and reasoning for an ordinary moral agent? For instance, do you need to calculate overall happiness by assigning a definite number to each person's happiness and apply some very complicated mathematical operation on these numbers?
(d) Does it require unrealistic motivational capacities, for instance, does it require ordinary agents to be like Jesus?

I am not claiming that this list is exhaustive. Some would perhaps like to add that an acceptable moral theory should be impartial. But I think this list captures the least controversial test questions. In fact, the theoretical questions seem important when we are doing non-moral theorizing as well, that is, scientific theorizing. Note also that the theoretical and practical questions are related. If a moral theory fails in clarity, simplicity, and internal coherence, it will be difficult to apply in real life.

The most controversial test question is no doubt the one about moral coherence. Can we justify a moral theory by pointing out that it coheres with our own favourite moral opinions? Is this not to favour the status quo? No, the aim is to make your moral beliefs coherent and no moral belief is sacred. It is just that the only sensible starting point is your own considered beliefs. The alternative, as Frank Jackson puts it, would be to 'start from somewhere unintuitive and that can hardly be a good place to start'.[2] But this does not prevent that, after a thorough reflection you may realize in the end that some of your initial judgements must be rejected.

In this book, I will frequently refer to these test questions when I am discussing a particular aspect of utilitarianism. Since it might be impossible to find a theory that scores high on all factors, we will have to be prepared to make difficult trade-offs and decide when a certain vice is compensated for by a certain virtue. This is especially true for moral coherence. It seems doubtful that there is a moral theory that matches all our considered moral judgements. This means that we may have to give up at least some of our pet moral convictions in order to make our moral beliefs coherent. Because of this, I have to warn you that doing normative ethics sincerely is a painful business. When judging the merits and demerits of utilitarianism you will find out what your own pet convictions imply and whether they form a coherent whole, and I can assure you that you will not always be happy about these findings. It is easy to convince yourself that your moral theory, whether utilitarian or non-utilitarian, is without problems if you consider only a narrow range of cases that happen to suit the theory well. But it is of course insincere to consider only the nice aspects of your moral beliefs and ignore the less attractive features. On a more positive note, thinking about these questions will help you to gain moral self-understanding by forcing you to consider the plausibility and coherence of your own moral views.

SUGGESTED READING

On the distinction between criterion of rightness and decision methods:

Bales, R. E. (1971), 'Act utilitarianism: Account of right-making characteristics or decision making procedure', *American Philosophical Quarterly*, Vol. 8, 257–265.

Bergström, L. (1996), 'Reflections on consequentialism', *Theoria*, Vol. LXII, Part 1–2.

Sidgwick, H. (1907), *The Methods of Ethics*, seventh edition, London: Macmillan, 78, 119, 121.

Tännsjö, T. (1995), 'In defence of theory in ethics', *Canadian Journal of Philosophy*, 25.

On how to assess normative theories:

Glover, J. (1977), *Causing Deaths and Saving Lives*, London: Penguin, Chapter 2.

Hooker, B. (2000), *Ideal Code, Real World*, Oxford: Oxford University Press, Chapter 1, Sections 1.2 –1.8.

Timmons, M. (2002), *Moral Theory: An Introduction*, New York: Rowman and Littlefield, Chapter 1.

CHAPTER THREE

WHAT IS UTILITARIANISM?

As I said in Chapter One, one of the basic tenets of utilitarianism is that we should make the world as good as we can and that we can only do this by making the lives of people as good as we can. On the face of it, this seems hard to deny. It seems implausible to claim that we ought to do *less* good than we can and that the world is *not* made better if people are made better off. So how come utilitarianism is such a controversial theory when it can sound so trivial and obviously true?

The answer is that we have to give a more precise definition of the theory in order to see its true implications. Vaguely expressed, many moral theories look reasonable. In this chapter, I shall start by taking utilitarianism apart and examine its basic elements one by one. I shall then give a brief introduction to the major competitors to utilitarianism. This will give you a feel for what utilitarianism rules out, and thus a better understanding of utilitarianism itself, but it will also provide you with some background knowledge that will be needed later on when we assess utilitarianism by comparing it to alternative moral theories.

THE BASIC ELEMENTS OF UTILITARIANISM

Suppose you want to know what you ought to do. How would a classical utilitarian answer this query? First, he would need to identify your *options*, the actions available to you at the time of choice. Second, he would need to identify the consequences of each of these actions.

Now, it is important to bear in mind that when utilitarians talk about 'the consequences of an action' they usually have in mind something more than just the causal effects of the action. In fact, they usually have in mind everything that would happen or be the case, if the action were performed. This will of course include the causal effects of the action, but many other things as well. Indeed, it will include the *whole possible world* that would be the case if the action were performed. In particular, it will include the action itself, because the action itself is trivially one of the things that would happen if the action were performed. Why should we adopt such an inclusive notion of outcome? Because otherwise important factors may be left out. For example, if one of your options is to torture someone for an hour and if we want to judge your act of torture by its consequences (and those of your alternative actions), we had better count the action itself as part of its relevant consequences. Otherwise, we would not be able to take into account the terrible suffering that this act of torture would *consist* in, only what would happen *after* the act of torture as a causal effect of this act.

Now, when we have identified your options and their respective outcomes, the utilitarian would evaluate each outcome by how much well-being it contains. The best outcome is the outcome that contains the greatest total sum of well-being. Or, more exactly:

Sum-ranking
One outcome is better than another if and only if it contains a greater total sum of well-being.[1]

This principle may sound pretty straightforward, but there are some hidden complications.

First, what does well-being consist in, that is, what makes a person's life better in itself for him? The classical utilitarian would say that it consists in subjective states, but which subjective states? The *hedonist* would say that pleasure is good for us and displeasure is bad for us, while the *desire-theorist* would say that it is the satisfaction of our desires that is good for us and the frustration of our desires that is bad for us. It is important to note that these views of well-being are not just about human well-being. Many non-human animals will count as having well-being, since they can feel pleasure and desire things. Recall Bentham's credo: 'the question is not, Can they *reason*? nor, Can they *talk*? but, Can they *suffer*?'[2]

Second, what do we mean by 'the greatest total sum of well-being'? The total sum of well-being contained in an outcome is arrived at in the following way. Assume for simplicity hedonism, the idea that only pleasures are good for us and only displeasures are bad for us. Take an individual who exists in the outcome. Go through all her pleasures and assign a positive value to each according to how intense the pleasure is. Sum these values. Go through all her displeasures and assign a negative value to each according to how intense the displeasure is. Then sum the pleasure values and the displeasure values. Repeat this procedure for all individuals in the outcome, and then sum their lifetime values. This is the total sum of well-being contained in the outcome.

Note that this means that sum-ranking expresses a kind of *impartiality*: Only the intensity and duration of a pleasure matter for the value of a pleasure and the value of an outcome containing this pleasure. The identity of the person feeling pleasure does not matter. So, my pleasure cannot be given extra weight just because I am Krister Bykvist. As Bentham succinctly put it: 'Everyone is to count for one, no one for more than one.'

Now, when we have decided how to evaluate the outcomes of your actions the utilitarian would tell you to perform the action that would have the best outcome. Or, more exactly:

> You *ought* to perform an action if and only if its outcome would be better than the outcome of any alternative action available to you.

This is one part of *maximizing act-consequentialism*. The other parts are:

> It is *right (permissible)* for you to perform an action if and only if its outcome would not be worse than the outcome of any alternative action.

> It is *wrong* for you to perform an action if and only if its outcome would be worse than the outcome of some alternative action available to you.

We can now state classical utilitarianism more exactly as follows by putting together sum-ranking and maximizing act-consequentialism:

Classical utilitarianism
An action ought to be done if and only if its outcome contains a sum total of (subjective) well-being that is greater than that which is contained in the outcome of any alternative action.

Classical utilitarianism provides us thus with a *criterion of rightness*, that is, a necessary and sufficient condition for ascribing a certain normative status to an action. It tells us what makes actions right or wrong, but it should not be seen as a decision method that should always be followed in deliberation. This was already clear to Bentham, who wrote: 'It is not to be expected that this process [calculating how much overall well-being each action will bring about] should be strictly pursued previously to every moral judgment, or to every legislative or judicial operation.'[3] Nor does classical utilitarianism ask agents to adopt certain moral motives. As Mill pointed out, that would be 'to mistake the very meaning of a standard of morals, and to confound the rule of action with the motive of it. It is the business of ethics to tell us what are our duties, or by what test we can know them, but no system of ethics requires that the sole motive of all we do shall be a feeling of duty [. . .]'.[4]

Note also that classical utilitarianism is a *universal* moral theory. It is meant to apply to *all* moral agents in *all* situations. Finally, note that it is an *act*-oriented utilitarian theory. It determines the rightness of an action by looking at the values of outcomes of *individual* acts. We can imagine other forms of utilitarianism according to which the rightness of an action is determined indirectly by the values of the outcome of something that is not an individual action: a rule under which the action is subsumed, for instance, or a motive from which the action springs. Classical utilitarianism is thus a form of act-utilitarianism. In the following, I will skip this qualification and simply refer to the theory as 'utilitarianism'. We will come back to indirect forms of utilitarianism in Chapter Ten.

To sum up in more succinct terms, the whole family of utilitarian theories is captured by the equation:

Utilitarianism = Consequentialism (nothing but the values of outcomes matter for the rightness of actions) + Welfarism (nothing but well-being matters for the value of outcomes)

Classical utilitarianism is captured by the following equation:

Classical utilitarianism = Maximizing act-consequentialism + Sum-ranking + Subjective conception of well-being

The elements of classical utilitarianism will be critically examined in the following chapters. The subjective conception of well-being and welfarism will be discussed in Chapter Four, sum-ranking in Chapter Five. Chapters Six to Ten will focus on some troublesome moral implications of classical utilitarianism, which have to do with maximizing act-consequentialism, welfarism, or both.

HISTORICAL BACKGROUND

Even though this is not a book on the history of utilitarianism, we cannot discuss it without mentioning its founders: Jeremy Bentham, John Stuart Mill, and Henry Sidgwick. As I said in the introduction, I will not give a separate treatment of their ideas but instead try to work their ideas and arguments into the general discussion to follow.

What I want to stress here is that not all of these founders of utilitarianism explicitly and consistently embraced what I have called classical utilitarianism. To see this, consider the slogan often attributed to Bentham: 'the greatest happiness to the greatest number is the measure of right and wrong'. On the face of it, this seems to give independent weight to the sheer number of recipients of happiness. Total happiness is not the only important thing; it also matters how many people are benefited. In a choice between two outcomes that contain the same amount of total happiness, we should realize the one in which more people are benefited.

Jeremy Bentham also wrote:

> By the principle of utility is meant that principle which approves or disapproves of every action whatsoever, according to the tendency which it appears to have to augment or diminish the happiness of the party whose interest is in question: or, what is the same thing in other words, to promote or to oppose that happiness.[5]

This seems to suggest that an action *should be approved of more strongly* if it tends to produce more happiness, not that we *ought to do* what will produce most happiness. But he also says, which comes closer to my definition:

> Of an action that is conformable to the principle of utility one may say either that it is one that ought to be done, or at least, that it is not one that ought not to be done.[6]

It comes closer, but not close enough, since it still differs in that it seems to suggest that the action that maximizes total well-being is only permissible, not necessarily obligatory.

Not even Mill, who took great pains in introducing utilitarianism to the general audience, gives a clear-cut formulation of classical utilitarianism. His famous definition of utilitarianism states that:

> [. . .] actions are right in proportion as they tend to promote happiness, wrong as they tend to produce the reverse of happiness.

This definition differs from classical utilitarianism in that it suggests that rightness comes in degree – that one action can be 'righter' than another – and that it does not explicitly state that one ought to maximize overall well-being. However, on a charitable interpretation, *the* right action, the one we ought to perform, can be identified with the action that is 'the most right and the least wrong', that is, the action that produces the greatest balance of well-being over ill-being.

Sidgwick comes pretty close to my definition of classical utilitarianism when he says that:

> [b]y Utilitarianism is here meant the ethical theory, that the conduct which, under any given circumstances, is objectively right, is that which will produce the greatest amount of happiness on the whole.[7]

This comes pretty close to my definition if 'objectively right' is understood as the uniquely right action, that is, the obligatory action. Yet, a striking difference remains between Sidgwick's and my definition: the values of outcomes are not explicitly mentioned. Recall that in my formulations of classical utilitarianism rightness is determined by outcome-values which are determined by what is good for people, which in turn is determined by subjective mental states. In contrast, according to the quotes from Bentham, Mill, and Sidgwick, what we should do is determined *directly* by facts about happiness. In fact, it was not until the writings of G. E. Moore that utilitarianism was explicitly defined as a form of consequentialism.[8]

So why call a theory *classical* utilitarianism when it is not clear that the utilitarian forefathers embraced it? Well, it is hard to find a clear and coherent picture of utilitarianism in the work of these writers.

Some formulations come close to my definition of classical utilitarianism but others, as we have seen, suggest a different theory. This should not come as a surprise since they were the first to think about utilitarianism in a more systematic way. It takes some time and effort to get things straight. Classical utilitarianism, as I define it, is therefore better seen as a *paradigm*, an *ideal type*. We will discuss various departures from this ideal type in the following chapters.

THE APPEAL OF UTILITARIANISM

Before I start bashing classical utilitarianism, I would like to say something in favour of it in order to show that it is a moral theory we should take seriously. Let us start by listing its theoretical virtues.

(a) Clarity

Assuming a clear understanding of the crucial notions of alternative actions, outcomes, value, and well-being, utilitarianism is a precise moral theory which, given appropriate empirical information, has clear implications for all moral choice situations.

(b) Simplicity

It consists of only *one* fundamental moral principle and thus avoids the complexity of pluralistic theories, which consist of a number of different principles. Consequently, the utilitarian need not worry about how to rank different principles in cases of conflict.

(c) Explanatory power

The range of actions explained by utilitarianism is vast. It assigns normative status (rightness or wrongness) to all options in all choice situations, including new choice situations that we had previously not considered as serious possibilities. There will be no 'normative gaps', actions that cannot be said to be obligatory, permissible, or wrong.

(d) Internal coherence

Utilitarianism is logically coherent; it will never say that an action is both overall right and overall wrong, since no action can have an outcome that is both better than that of any alternative action and worse than that of some alternative action.

(e) Moral coherence

Utilitarianism seems to square well with many of our considered particular judgements. For instance, it agrees with common sense that the number of lives counts. If two lifeboats are sinking and we only have time to rescue the people from one of the boats, we should go for the larger group. Similarly, if the crashing airplane can be steered towards a less crowded part of the city, that is what the pilot should do.

Utilitarianism will also embrace some of our considered general judgements. For instance, if one outcome contains less suffering than another, then that is a reason to bring about the former outcome. Of course, utilitarianism differs from common sense in that it *only* gives weight to happiness and suffering and no weight to other factors. The only reason we can have for choosing one outcome over another is that the former contains more happiness or less suffering.

(f) Consistent prescriptions

Among the practical virtues of utilitarianism, we could mention the fact that it will always give us prescriptions that can be followed. Utilitarianism will never entail that we ought to do something and we ought to refrain from doing it. This seems to be a plus, since theories that give inconsistent prescriptions cannot be action guiding. 'You ought to do A and you ought to refrain from doing A' is not a useful piece of advice.

In addition to these general theoretical and practical virtues, utilitarianism can also be seen as expressing or embodying important features that seem constitutive of morality:

(1) *It captures one of the ways we should respond to the good and the bad.*
Utilitarianism accepts the consequentialist prescription to maximize the good, and to minimize the evil. This is a plus, since it is odd to say that we are permitted to do less good than we can.

(2) *The ideal moral agent is seen as an impartial benevolent spectator.*
Impartiality seems to be an important mark of the moral outlook. Moral conflicts should be solved from an impartial standpoint where no person is singled out and given more weight. After all, this detached attitude is what we expect in people who occupy important

public positions in society. For instance, it is the attitude we expect in a judge who has to decide whether the accused is guilty and what punishment to administer. A judge who favours herself and her nearest and dearest would not elicit moral admiration.

Utilitarianism can embrace this idea of impartiality. The ideal utilitarian agent resembles an impartial judge since he evaluates the situation objectively and from the 'outside'. He wishes people well without identifying and participating emotionally. No person is singled out and given more weight. For instance, he does not give more weight to the happiness of a person because it is *his* happiness, or *his* parents' happiness. An ordinary person can approximate this perspective by detaching herself from her personal engagement in the situation.

Many people would, however, argue that this detachment tells against utilitarianism. This form of utilitarianism is flawed precisely because the personal point of view is lost. The ideal moral attitude is not one of detachment, but one of engagement and emotional participation. The following alternative model of utilitarianism acknowledges the importance of emotional participation.

(3) *The ideal moral agent shows generalized self-concern.*

The ideal moral agent is someone who identifies with other subjects and imaginatively puts herself in the other person's situation. The 'situation' here is supposed to include not just the other person's external circumstances and physical features but also her feelings and preferences. You can approximate this ideal by asking how you would feel about being in the other person's situation. So, if you succeed in this identification, you will view things from other people's perspectives and the objects of their preferences will present themselves as attractive to you.

How will it work more exactly? I will just give a rough sketch.[9] Suppose that you want a parking space and wonder whether to move someone else's bicycle in order to park your car. Assume that the other person does not want to move her bicycle. No other persons are involved. How are we to solve this conflict on the participant model? Identify with the other person. Then you will see things from her perspective and see the attractiveness of not moving the bicycle. Remember that you are supposed to identify in the strong sense of taking over other people's preferences. Now, when you see both the attractiveness of parking the car there and the attractiveness of not moving the bicycle what should you do? Compare the *intensities* of your preference for parking the car with the intensity of your newly acquired preference for not moving the bicycle and then satisfy the stronger preference of the two. So, in a way, conflicts *between* persons are reduced to conflicts *within* persons.

ALTERNATIVES TO UTILITARIANISM

Since one of the main aims of this book is to evaluate utilitarianism, not in isolation, but in comparison with other non-utilitarian theories, I need to introduce the main competitors to utilitarianism. Of course, since this book is only a short introduction to utilitarianism, I will not be able to go into detail. However, even though what follows is no more than a thumbnail sketch of the main competitors, I think it is enough to give you a feeling of what utilitarianism rules out.

NON-UTILITARIAN CONSEQUENTIALISM

A non-utilitarian consequentialist judges actions by the value of their outcomes but denies that well-being is all that matters for the value of an outcome. This opens up a wide range of options. For instance, inequality can be seen as intrinsically bad and freedom can be seen as intrinsically good. Even intentions and actions can be assigned intrinsic value. Evil intentions and evil actions, such as sadistic torture, can be judged intrinsically bad. In principle, any state of affairs can be assigned intrinsic value. Non-utilitarian consequentialism is thus not itself a moral theory. It is better seen as a family of moral theories whose members differ radically from each other with respect to what is judged valuable and thus worth promoting.

DEONTOLOGICAL THEORIES

'Deontology' is a slippery term that can be used to mean different things. When people talk about deontological theories they usually have in mind moral theories that deny consequentialism and thus deny that all that matter for rightness are the values of outcomes. However, they need not deny that outcome-values matter. It is just that they think that there are other factors that are relevant to moral rightness. In particular, they think that it matters a great deal *how* and *why* outcomes are brought about. For instance, many deontologists think that there is a morally relevant distinction between doing harm and allowing harm. Doing harm is worse than allowing harm, so it can be permissible to allow harm but impermissible to actively bring about the same kind of harm. For instance, it can be permissible to allow starving people in developing countries to die even though it is impermissible to kill them by sending them poisoned food.

Another distinction that is often endorsed by deontologists is the one between intending harm and foreseeing harm. A harm is intended when it is aimed at as an end or as a means to some other end. A harm is merely foreseen when it is a known but unintended consequence of an action. This distinction is then used as the basis for the double-effect doctrine, which says, roughly, that it is wrong to harm *in order* to bring about something good, but it is permissible to bring about some good, *foreseeing* that it will lead to harm.

Utilitarians will of course deny these distinctions since for them all that matters is that total well-being is promoted; it does not matter how and why it is promoted.

KANTIANISM

Kantianism is a form of deontology where intentions and motives play a significant role. Again, this *–ism* is more of a family of related theories than a particular theory. Kant's own writing contains a wealth of different principles and it is not always easy to see what the principles amount to and how they are supposed to hang together. Even though Kantians differ in what they think are the most central principles and how they should be interpreted, they often give a prominent place to the principle of universalization and the Humanity principle.

The principle of universalization, or, as Kant himself dubbed it, the Categorical Imperative in its universal law form, can be seen as a version of the universalization test we so often invoke in moral debates: 'What would happen if everyone thought that it was OK to evade taxes?' The Kantian version is 'Could you consistently and rationally will that everyone thinks it is OK to evade taxes?' Note that the focus is on consistent and rational willing rather than the value of the consequences of everyone thinking it OK to do these things. A more exact formulation of the Kantian universalization principle is the following:

It is permissible for you to act on a certain maxim if and only if you can consistently and rationally will that everyone act on it.

A maxim is an individual plan or policy, for example, 'Whenever I borrow something from a friend, I shall return it'.

To apply the universalization principle you have to go through the following three-step procedure:

(1) Identify the maxim of your action.
(2) Imagine that everyone is acting on your maxim.
(3) Consider whether you could consistently and rationally will that everyone acts on your maxim.

Steps (1) and (2) are fairly obvious, but step (3) needs to be clarified a bit more. To give you a feel of what can or cannot be consistently and rationally willed, consider these two maxims:

(a) Whenever I borrow something from my friend, I shall return it.
(b) Whenever I need some work done, I shall enslave you.

Maxim (a) can be consistently willed since it is perfectly coherent to imagine that everyone is acting on it. Maxim (b), however, is more problematic, since if this maxim were acted on by both of us in a situation in which each needs some work done, I would be your slave and you would be my slave, and that seems incoherent.

The universalization principle would thus say that acting on (a) is permissible, but acting on (b) is impermissible.

The Humanity principle is easier to formulate:

It is wrong to treat a person merely as a means.
It is right to treat a person as an end.

It is important to note the qualification 'merely' here. The Humanity principle does not say that it is wrong for you to use people and their services. You do that all the time when you interact with shopkeepers, bank managers, and so on. But you do not treat them merely as a means (I hope). Now, the Humanity principle certainly sounds very attractive. No one denies that we should not treat people as tools and resources to be used at our own discretion. But, as we shall see in Chapter Nine, it is in fact quite difficult to spell out the crucial notion of treating someone as an end.[10]

VIRTUE ETHICS

Virtue ethics is a family of moral theories that are united by the fundamental role they give to the virtues of people. The most fundamental moral question is therefore, 'What kind of person ought I to be?' rather than 'Which particular action ought I to perform?' Some virtue ethicists even go so far as to say that the question about what we morally ought to do is misconceived. Other virtue ethicists are less extreme. They claim that it does make sense to talk about what we morally ought to do. But what we morally ought to do is explained by facts about virtues.

There are different views on how to explain moral rightness in terms of virtues. One popular view is:

(a) An action is right for an agent if and only if a fully virtuous person would do it.

As it stands, this principle does not say much until we have made clear what we mean by a 'fully virtuous person'.

One idea would be to define a virtuous person as someone who is disposed to perform morally right actions. But this will not work since then the theory would become circular: what makes an action right is that it would be performed by a virtuous person, but what makes a person virtuous is that he is disposed to do what is morally right.

A better suggestion is that a virtuous person should be seen as someone who is disposed to benefit others. But then (a) would say that an action is right just in case it would be done by a person who is disposed to benefit others. But this comes close to a form of utilitarianism. Another option would be to say that what makes an action right is that it would be done by someone who is disposed to treat people as ends. But this seems to be a Kantian theory in disguise. So on either of the suggested readings, virtue ethics would not come out as a distinct moral theory.

Is there any way we can define a virtuous person so that the principle neither becomes circular nor collapses into utilitarianism or deontology?

Here is one way of doing it. It seems obvious that a virtuous person is someone who has all the virtues. A virtue is some kind of relatively fixed character trait, involving dispositions to think, feel, and act in certain ways. Aristotle would add that they have to be habitually formed and maintained, and not just natural traits we were lucky to have been born with. But what are the virtues? If we trust common sense, we would list things such as courage, benevolence, honesty, and justice. This seems to give us a theory with some content: what explains that an action is right is that it would be done by a person who is courageous, benevolent, honest, just, and so on. But the problem is that it only gives us an 'unconnected heap of virtues'. What is missing is some unified explanation of what makes a character trait a virtue.

The Aristotelian conception of virtues offers such an account. Virtues are character traits that are essential to a good human life. You need to act virtuously in order to flourish as a human. A flourishing life is thus not just a life that is useful for other people; it is a life that benefits the person who leads the life. It is important to stress that when we talk about benefits here, we are not just talking about subjective benefits in terms of pleasure or desire satisfaction. The idea is rather that something important is missing in a life that is full of pleasure and desire satisfaction but lacking in admirable character traits and deeds.

Some virtue ethicists are not happy with (a) because on this account a right action need not express any virtues of the agent. It is enough that the action *would* have been performed by a virtuous person. To close the gap between right actions and displayed virtues, they instead propose the following principle:

(b) An action is right for an agent if and only if the agent would do it from a virtuous motive (or the most virtuous motive available to the agent).

This principle makes sure that when you act rightly you express some virtuous motive. If virtues are defined as what makes a human life flourish, a harmony between morality and human good is created: when you act rightly, you benefit yourself by making your life a better human life.

SUGGESTED READING

On the definitions of utilitarianism and consequentialism:

Bentham, J. (1823), *The Principles of Morals and Legislation*, London: T. Payne (originally printed 1789), Chapter 1.

Bykvist, K. (2003), 'Normative supervenience and consequentialism', *Utilitas*, March, Vol. 15, No.1, 27–48.
Carlson, E. (1995), *Consequentialism Reconsidered*, Dordrecht: Kluwer, Chapter 2.
Mill, J. S. (1871), *Utilitarianism*, London: Longmans, Green, Reader & Dyer, Chapters 1 and 2.
Moore, G. E. (1912), *Ethics*, Oxford: Oxford University Press, Chapters 1–2.
Scheffler, S., (ed.), (1991), *Consequentialism and Its Critics*, Oxford: Oxford University Press, Introduction.
Sen A. and Williams, B., (eds.), (1982), *Utilitarianism and Beyond*, Cambridge: Cambridge University Press, Introduction.
Tännsjö, T. (1998), *Hedonistic Utilitarianism*, Edinburgh: Edinburgh University Press, Chapter 3.

On utilitarianism as detached impartial benevolence:

Rabinowicz, W. and Österberg, J. (1996), 'Value based on preferences: On two interpretations of preference utilitarianism', *Economics and Philosophy*, Vol. 12, 1–27, esp. Österberg's part of the paper.

On utilitarianism as generalized self-concern:

Hare, R. M. (1981), *Moral Thinking*, Oxford: Clarendon Press.
Rabiniwicz, W. and Österberg, J. (1996), 'Value based on preferences: On two interpretations of preference utilitarianism', *Economics and Philosophy*, Vol. 12, 1–27, esp. Rabinowicz' part of the paper.

On the history of utilitarianism:

Crisp, R. (1997), *Mill on Utilitarianism*, Routledge Philosophy Guidebooks, London: Routledge.
Kelly, P. J. (1990), *Utilitarianism and Distributive Justice: Jeremy Bentham and the Civil Law*. Oxford: Oxford University Press.
Schultz, B., (ed.), (1992), *Essays on Henry Sidgwick*, New York: Cambridge University Press.

On deontological theories, general:

Kagan, S. (1989), *The Limits of Morality*, Oxford: Oxford University Press, Chapters 1–2.
Kamm, F. (2007), *Intricate Ethics*, Oxford: Oxford University Press, Chapter 1.
Ross, W. D. (1930), *The Right and the Good*, Oxford: Clarendon Press, Chapter 2.

On acts and omissions:

Foot, P. (1978), 'The problem of abortion and the doctrine of double effect', in her *Virtues and Vices*, Berkeley, CA: University of California Press.

Glover, J. (1977), *Causing Deaths and Saving Lives*, London: Penguin, Chapter 7.

Kagan, S. (1989), *The Limits of Morality*, Oxford: Oxford University Press, Chapter 3.

On intended effects and foreseen effects:

Foot, P. (1978), 'The problem of abortion and the doctrine of double effect', in Foot, P., (ed.), *Virtues and Vices*, Berkeley, CA: University of California Press, 19–32.

Glover, J. (1977), *Causing Deaths and Saving Lives*, London: Penguin, Chapter 6.

Kagan, S. (1989), *The Limits of Morality*, Oxford: Oxford University Press, Chapter 4.

On Kant's ethics:

Hill, T. (1991), *Autonomy and Self-Respect*, Cambridge: Cambridge University Press.

Kant, I. (1948), *Groundwork of the Metaphysics of Morals*, trans. Paton H. J., London: Hutchinson, (Originally published in 1785).

Korsgaard, C. (1996), *Creating the Kingdom of Ends*, Cambridge: Cambridge University Press, Part 1.

O'Neill, O. (1989), *Constructions of Reason*, Cambridge: Cambridge University Press, Chapter 5.

On Neo-Kantians:

Baron, M. (1997), 'Kantian ethics', in Baron, M., Pettit, P. and Slote, M., (eds.), *Three Methods of Ethics*, Oxford: Blackwell, 3–91.

Korsgaard, C. (1996), *The Sources of Normativity*, Cambridge: Cambridge University Press.

O'Neill, O. (1989), *Constructions of Reason*, Cambridge: Cambridge University Press.

On Aristotelian virtue ethics:

Aristotle, *Nicomachean Ethics*, Book 1, Book 2 Chapters 1–7, Book 6 Chapters 9–11, Book 7 Chapters 1–10.

Sherman N., (ed.), (1999), *Aristotle's ethics. Critical Essays,* Lanham, Maryland: Rowman and Littlefield.

Urmson, J. (1988), *Aristotle's Ethics*, Oxford: Blackwell, Chapters 2 and 6.

On modern virtue theory:

Crisp, R. (1996), 'Modern moral philosophy and the virtues', in Crisp, R., (ed.), *How Should One Live?*, Oxford: Clarendon Press, 1–18.

Foot, P. (1978), *Virtues and Vices*, Oxford: Blackwell.

Hursthouse, R. (1996), 'Normative virtue ethics', in Crisp, R., (ed.), *How Should One Live?*, Oxford: Clarendon Press, 19–36.
Schneewind, J. B. (1997), 'The misfortunes of virtue', in Crisp, R. and Slote, M., (eds.), *Virtue Ethics*, Oxford: Oxford University Press, 78–200.

CHAPTER FOUR

WELL-BEING

One of the crucial components of utilitarianism is welfarism, the view that nothing but the well-being of people and animals matter for the values of outcomes. To see what this commitment amounts to we need to clarify what well-being consists in. In this chapter, I will therefore discuss the pros and cons of the utilitarian conception of well-being, which states, roughly, that well-being consists in subjective states of people and animals. This conception of well-being can be spelled out in two distinct ways. According to the desire theory, what is good for a person is the satisfaction of his desires, what is bad, the frustration of his desires. According to hedonism, however, only pleasure is good for a person, and only displeasure bad. The main question in this chapter is whether the utilitarian conception of well-being holds water as a well-being theory in its own right, but I will also assess some of its moral implications.

THE CONCEPT OF WELL-BEING

A person's welfare or well-being concerns what is good *for* him, what makes his life worth living. It therefore depends crucially on facts about the person and his life. As William James jokingly remarked, whether a life is worth living depends on the *liver*.[1] To give you a better idea of what I mean by well-being, consider the crib test presented by Feldman and Darwall.[2] Imagine that you are filled with love as you look into the crib, checking on your newborn baby boy. Your concern for the baby expresses itself in the hope that things will turn out well for him, that he will have a life that is good *in itself for* him.

This is not the same as hoping that he will have a morally good life. Your baby boy might turn out to be a morally admirable person with a benevolent heart and a strong sense of justice, but it is possible that he will simply be too well-behaved for his own good. Suppose, for instance, that his fight against injustice and poverty leads him to constantly sacrifice his own good for the sake of others.

Nor is it the same as hoping that he will lead an aesthetically admirable life. Your baby boy might turn out to be a great artist, but, again, this need not guarantee a life that is good for him, for it is possible that his artistic life will be marred with bad health, self-doubt, and lack of social recognition. Hence, we should not confuse well-being with moral or aesthetic value.

THEORIES OF WELL-BEING

Before we begin our critical assessment of the subjective conception of well-being, we need to get clearer about the nature of a well-being theory. A substantive well-being theory is more than a list of *what* is good for and what is bad for people (and animals). It also provides an explanation of *why* some things are good for us and some things are bad for us. For instance, the hedonist is not just saying that your pleasant experiences are good for you, but also that what *makes* your pleasant experience good for you is the fact that it feels pleasant to you. Similarly, a desire theory is not just saying that the things you desire are good for you; it is also saying that what *makes* something good for you is the fact that it is desired by you. In this way, a substantive theory of well-being is similar to a substantive normative theory, which is not just providing a list of rights and wrongs but also an explanation of why rights are right and wrongs are wrong.

As with right-makers, good-for-makers need not in fact make something *overall* good for you. The fact that the present moment of your life contains pleasure is, according to the hedonist, something that makes the moment good for you in one respect. But this does not mean that the moment is overall good for you, since it may also contain some displeasure, which is something that makes the moment bad for you in one respect. To decide whether the moment is overall good for you, we need to weigh the pleasures against the displeasures.

Another common feature of substantive well-being theories and normative theories is that they do not provide definitions of terms and concepts. For instance, to say, with the hedonist, that my present moment is good for me because it contains more pleasure than pain is not to say that 'my life contains more pleasure than pain' means the same as 'my life is good for me'.

With these distinctions at hand, we can easily pinpoint the difference between subjective and objective conceptions of well-being. Whereas the subjective conception claims that what makes something good for a person is always a fact about the person's psychological states, the objective conception denies this and claims instead that some objective states of a person can make something good for the person.

Unfortunately, this way of drawing the distinction is not always adopted in the contemporary debate on well-being. For instance, it is common to be told that subjective accounts hold that *what* is good for people is something subjective. But this is to confuse the nature of the bearers of well-being – what is good for people – with the nature of the good-for-makers. Even in a subjective account these can come apart. For instance, according to the desire theory, something objective can be good for me – say, my physical health – but it is good for me because I desire it.

Furthermore, it is common to conflate substantive accounts with conceptual accounts of well-being. It is common to be told that desire theory holds that the notion of being good for me should be analyzed as desired by me. But this is not a substantive view of well-being, since it does not say what makes something good for me. Let me explain. What makes something good for you must be something different from the property of being good for you. Otherwise we would have a fact that explains itself: the fact that something is good for you explains why it is good for you. So goodness for you is one thing, what explains it, another. If it is true that goodness for you should be analyzed as desired by you, then what makes something good for you will be the feature in virtue of which you desire it, not goodness for you itself.

It is also important to note that a substantive well-being theory is about what is good *in itself* for a person. It is not in the business of providing a list of *sources* of well-being. A source of well-being is something that tends to lead to something that is good in itself for a person. Different substantive well-being theories can agree on a list of well-being sources. For instance, both hedonists and desire theorists can agree that health, education, and safety are crucial sources of well-being, since they tend to lead to both pleasure and desire satisfaction.

HEDONISM

In analogy with substantive theories of rightness, many substantive theories of well-being can be cashed out as a *criterion* of well-being of the following form:

> x is good for you if and only if x is F.
> x is bad for you if and only if x is G.

Hedonism seems to fit this mould, since it could be formulated more exactly as:

> x is good for you if and only if x contains more of your pleasure than displeasure.
> x is bad for you if and only if x contains more of your displeasure than pleasure.

PROBLEMS FOR HEDONISM

False pleasures

One of the most controversial slogans of hedonism is 'what you don't feel can't harm or benefit you'. It has a ring of truth, no doubt, since we do say things like this to our friends to alleviate their anxiety over some hidden facts about their lives. But the slogan is difficult to accept when you think more about pleasures that are based on false beliefs. Suppose, for instance, that you are hooked up to an experience machine that stimulates your brain so that you feel as if you were writing a great novel, or making new friends, and reading an interesting book. In fact, since it simulates all the things you care about and value in life, you are guaranteed to feel constant pleasure and no displeasure. Would it be good for you to be hooked up to this machine for life, as good as living a real life with the same amount of pleasure? Would it not be bad for you in any respect?[3]

The hedonist seems forced to say 'yes' to both questions, at least if we assume that the machine will never malfunction. Since the machine gives you pleasures and no displeasures, the hedonist must say that your machine-life contains only good things and no bad things. But is this really the kind of life you would wish on your child when you look into the crib filled with love?

The hedonist could respond that our intuitions in this case are not reliable since machine lives are hard to grasp. However, we do not need to imagine experience machines to make the point. Consider the movie *The Truman Show*, which is about Truman who literally lives in a soap opera, surrounded by actors who pretend to be his caring parents, friends, girlfriends, and neighbours. Millions of people watch him every day. From the inside, his life looks and feels perfect, for he thinks he gets exactly what he wants. Do we think that he lives a good life, and that it is as good for him as a real life in which he gets what he wants and not just thinks he gets what he wants? Do we think that nothing bad happens to him, (assuming, in contrast to what happens in the movie, that he never gets to know the truth)?

We can press the same point with more down-to-earth examples, since, sadly, our own lives often look like a soap opera:

(a) I mistakenly think that my partner is faithful and feel very pleased.
(b) I mistakenly think that you are a good friend and feel very pleased.
(c) I mistakenly think that my parents love me and feel very pleased.
(d) I mistakenly think that I am not slandered behind my back and feel very pleased.

These cases all involve pleasures that are based on false beliefs. But for the hedonist, this cannot make them less valuable.

Well-being on a rainy day

Another troublesome implication of hedonism is that we are often wrong about how well off we are at particular moments and periods in our lives. Consider someone who 'has it all'. He is surrounded by loving and caring family members and friends, has a challenging but intellectually and emotionally rewarding job, and pursues worthwhile projects, often with great success. Now, intuitively we would like to say that even on an ordinary rainy day his well-being level is pretty high. But think about how flat his experiences are on such a day.

For long periods of time he feels neither strong pleasure, nor strong displeasure. Even though he knows that he has it all and his main desires are fulfilled, this is not something he is constantly thinking about during the day. Rather, he is immersed in the trivialities of life with its small ups and downs. According to hedonism, then, we would have to say that on a day like this his life is barely worth living. But this, surely, flies in the face of common sense. We would like to say that his well-being on such a day is pretty high, in any case, much greater than that of a pain-free but lonely patient who can only take mild pleasure in being fed and washed.

Of course, the hedonist could reply that we are conflating well-being *sources* with well-being itself. It is true, he would say, that in terms of well-being sources the successful person has it all; it is just that his great potential for pleasure is not realized on a dreary rainy day. In contrast, the bedridden lonely patient has very few well-being sources. The intuitive judgement that the patient is much worse off therefore stands, if we understand 'worse off' as 'worse off in terms of well-being sources'.

It is doubtful that this will satisfy the critic of hedonism. He would insist that the hedonist has an all too narrow view of what makes a life, or a day in a life, good for a person. It is true that small pleasures count for something. But to leave out all other factors, such as successful projects, intimate and loving relationships, is all too restrictive. The pain-free patient is therefore not just worse off in terms of well-being sources; he is worse off in terms of well-being.

ATTITUDINAL HEDONISM TO THE RESCUE?

A more general response to the objections we have considered so far would be to say that they rely on an all too narrow conception of pleasure. We have implicitly assumed that pleasure is nothing more than a pleasant sensation, an experience with a certain felt quality. It is this assumption that makes for problems in the false pleasure cases and the rainy-day case. Since it feels good to have a false pleasure, it must be good for you and cannot be bad for you in any respect. Similarly, since your life on a rainy day does not feel especially good, it cannot be especially good for you.

In response, the hedonist could claim that these troublesome implications can be avoided, if we adopt a wider conception of pleasure. But what would such a conception look like? How can pleasure be anything but an experience with a certain felt quality? Well, note that we sometimes talk about *taking pleasure in facts*. I can take pleasure in the fact that I have caring friends around, for instance. But when I take pleasure in this fact there must be such a fact for me to take pleasure in. So, if pleasure is seen as an attitude towards facts rather than a felt sensation, we can avoid the problems with false pleasures. For in these cases, I believe that my life contains certain facts, but, sadly, there are no such facts, so it is not true that I am taking pleasure in them. I only take pleasure in what I *believe* are facts about my life.

Note also that we can take great pleasure in things without feeling much pleasure. Just think of a car crash victim who has just woken up in the hospital bed. He can take pleasure in the fact that he survived the car crash even though the anesthetics take away all bodily sensations of pleasure and pain.[4] This means that, on a rainy day when things look and feel a bit grey I can still take great pleasure in the fact that I am successful in so many respects. It is just that I do not *feel* much pleasure.

Is this attitudinal hedonism a better version of hedonism? It is true that it avoids the difficulty with the rainy days, but it only partially answers the challenge set by false pleasures, for even if we no longer have to say that false pleasures must be good for a person, we still have to say that nothing bad is happening to a person who is living in an illusion. Nothing bad is happening to him because there is no fact of his life that he takes displeasure in. But are we willing to say that there are no bad things happening to Truman in his life? Similarly, are we willing to say that it is not bad for you to be deceived and slandered behind your back?

DESIRE-BASED THEORIES

It is here that desire theories step in. They would agree with the attitudinal hedonist that your well-being depends crucially on your attitudes towards facts, but they would identify these attitudes with desires rather than pleasure-takings. There is a crucial difference between desires and pleasure-takings: you can desire something without believing it to be the case, but you cannot take pleasure in something without believing it to be the case. 'I am now taking pleasure in playing the guitar but I do not believe I am playing the guitar' is incoherent. The desire theory could therefore claim that there are things that are bad for you even if these things are never believed to obtain. A life with false pleasures will be bad for you, since most of your desires are frustrated even though you do not know it. For instance, it is bad for you to be deceived and slandered behind your back since you desire not to be treated in these ways.

If the attitudinal hedonist wants to claim that these things are bad for you, he would have to reformulate his theory so that it says that it is bad for you to take pleasure in what you believe is the case when in fact it is not the case. But then, he would have drained hedonism of much of its content, since it now allows for bad things that do not involve any displeasure. Better, I think, to treat this theory as a version of the desire theory.

The desire theory will also give the right verdict on the lucky person who has it all. He has a pretty good life even on a rainy day, since his desires for having friends, love, and a challenging job are all satisfied even though he is not thinking about this during the day.

I have said that, according to the desire theory, it is bad for you to have frustrated desires, good for you to have satisfied desires. This is slightly misleading. Suppose you do not want to have a headache in the sense that you prefer not having a headache to having a headache. Then a desire theory seems forced to say that when this want is satisfied something positively good occurs in your life. It also seems forced to say that if you create anti-headache desires in order to satisfy them, you make your life better, other things being equal. But it seems much more sensible to say that the satisfactions of anti-headache desires are neutral for you, since, if you are like me, you take a *neutral* attitude towards not having a headache, and a negative attitude towards having a headache. Therefore, a properly formulated desire theory should say that it is good for you to get what you *favour*. Roughly put, to favour something is to be positively oriented towards it in your actions, emotions, feelings, or evaluative responses. So, if you have a positive attitude towards something, you tend to be motivated to bring it about, be glad and happy when you think it obtains, have pleasant thoughts about it, or see it in a good light.[5]

Similarly, whether it is bad for you to have a desire frustrated depends your attitude towards the absence of the desired object. Suppose that you want to get an unexpected gift, in the sense that you prefer getting the gift to not getting it, and that you take a neutral attitude towards not getting it. A sensible desire theory should then say that when this desire is frustrated nothing positively bad occurs in your life. Not getting this gift is instead neutral for you. So, it is not necessarily bad for you to have your desires frustrated. What is bad for you is to get what you *disfavour*. Roughly put, to disfavour something is to be negatively oriented towards it in your actions, emotions, feelings, or evaluative responses. You tend to be motivated to avoid it, be sad and unhappy when you think it obtains, have unpleasant thoughts about it, or see it in a bad light.[6]

The desire theory is therefore better formulated thus:

> x is good for you if and only if you favour x more than you disfavour it.
> x is bad for you if and only if you disfavour x more than you favour it.[7]

PROBLEMS FOR DESIRE-BASED THEORIES

All too narrow view of well-being?

One could object to the desire theory that it overreacts to the shortcomings of hedonism. It is true that it does better than hedonism in allowing goods and bads that are not experienced or believed to obtain. But it seems to go to the other extreme in denying that pleasures and pains are ever relevant to well-being, since it is only bare satisfactions and frustrations of desires that matter.

One obvious reaction to this objection is to adopt a pluralist theory that assigns value to both desire satisfactions and pleasures. But perhaps this reaction is premature; perhaps it fails to see the true potentials of the desire theory. It is true that, on this theory, what matters fundamentally are the satisfactions and frustrations of desires, but since we, typically, do favour pleasure and disfavour displeasure, it is normally good for us to feel pleasure and bad for us to feel displeasure. It is just that we also need to count other things we care about, things that go beyond the confines of our experiences and beliefs. In those cases where someone seems to favour having a painful experience – think of sadomasochism – it is not clear why this must be bad for him since he willingly engages in this activity. Furthermore, desires seem to play a crucial role in deciding whether a painful experience followed by a pleasurable experience is on the whole something good for us. If we could somehow establish that the intensity of the excruciating pain from running a marathon was greater than the intensity of the pleasure of winning the race, would that show that this was bad for you, if you nevertheless thought the pain was worth it and thus took a positive attitude towards this sequence of events?

Disinterested desires

My desire can be satisfied or frustrated without me being aware of it. As we have seen, it is exactly this feature that makes it possible for us to say that something bad is happening to the person who is experiencing false pleasures. However, many would argue that this feature also creates difficulties for the desire theory. To see this, suppose Carl Sagan wants us to establish contact with extraterrestrial beings.[8] Assume that 20,000 years from now we do establish contact with some alien civilization on some planet far away. Sagan's desire is thus satisfied but, sadly, he will never know anything about it. Since the satisfaction of this desire has no discernible effects on Sagan, how could it make his life go better? Or, to take another example, suppose that you want your brother to be cured from some debilitating disease.[9] Your brother is cured, but since you have lost contact with him, you will never know. How can this make your life better if you will never know about your brother's recovery?

I share these intuitions about these cases, but I doubt that they show that desire theory should be abandoned. What they show is rather that we should reject an unrestricted desire theory and introduce a 'personal constraint'. Since facts about your well-being are constituted by facts about you and your life, we should only count desires that range over facts about you and your life. Of course, it is not easy to pinpoint exactly what counts as a fact about you and your life, but it is at least clear that your desire is about you and your life *only if* it is about something that entails that you exist at some point in time. In both examples above, the desires of the person range over states of affairs that do not entail that he exists, and a personal constraint would therefore exclude them.

The relevance of this feature to our well-being is seen more clearly if we reconsider the examples of Sagan and your brother. Change the example of Sagan so that he now wants, not only that we meet aliens, but also, that *he helps to bring about* this meeting. Assume that he has been working for this goal during a major part of his life. Then it does not seem counter-intuitive to say that his well-being is increased by the satisfaction of this desire. What was counter-intuitive about counting Sagan's original desire was that it did not involve him. In the modified example, however, his desire clearly involves him, since his desire is that he plays an active part in bringing about the meeting. Consider also the example of your brother. Assume this time that you are a doctor who has worked for years to find a cure to your brother's disease and that you want, not just that your brother is cured, but also, that he is cured *by you*. Then, again, it does not seem odd to claim that satisfying this desire makes your life better. For in this case, your desire is about yourself, that is, that *you* cure your brother.

The right response to the problematic cases is not to move in the direction of hedonism and say that something can make a person better or worse off only if it enters or affects his experience in some way. What we should do is rather to impose a personal restriction and say that only desires that are about a person and his life can make him better or worse off.

Self-sacrifice

Another popular objection to the desire theory is to say that it implies that it is impossible to willingly sacrifice yourself for others. To willingly sacrifice yourself is to do something you want to do. But if you do what you want to do then, according to the desire theory, it must be good for you. So, it cannot be a sacrifice.

Again, I do not think that this threatens desire theory as such. A restricted version that incorporates a personal restriction will exclude *other-regarding* desires, since they are not about things that essentially involve the person. So, if your fundamental desire is *that Jane, Bob, and Henry live* and you satisfy this desire by throwing yourself on the hand-grenade that is threatening to kill them, you are not thereby made better off.

However, if we change the example so that your fundamental desire is that *you save your friends*, this move will no longer work. Satisfying this desire will be good for you, since it seems to essentially involve you. Does this show that your action is not a self-sacrifice? No, even if you satisfy one of your present desires by sacrificing your life, you still fail to satisfy many other desires, namely, all the future desires that would have been satisfied if you had not killed yourself now. Since your total well-being depends on all your desires, past, present, and future, there is no problem imagining that you do what you most want to do *now*, and still your action is not best for you on the whole.

Uninformed desires

Another problem for the desire theory is that many desires seem to be based on false beliefs and faulty reasoning, and it seems strange to say that satisfying these desires make you better off. Here are some popular examples:

(1) I have a choice between drinking a grey liquid and an orange one. I want to drink the orange one because I think it is tastier. But, as a matter of fact, it contains deadly poison.
(2) I have a choice between two treatments for cancer: A and B. I prefer B in the belief that this treatment will cure me. But, as a matter of fact, it will not. A would have cured me.
(3) I prefer the life of a philosopher to the life of a tennis player. I choose to pursue a career in philosophy but realize after a while that philosophy bores me to death.
(4) I prefer not enjoying myself too much because I mistakenly think that God disapproves of personal indulgence.

Satisfying these desires does not seem to be good for me. One obvious remedy would be to count only informed and rational desires, that is, desires that are based on true beliefs and correct reasoning. But one might wonder if this rationality constraint is necessary once we distinguish between intrinsic and instrumental desires. I have an intrinsic desire for something if I desire it as an end in itself, in virtue of what it is in itself. I have an instrumental desire for something if I desire it as a means to an end. For instance, my desire to not be in pain is an intrinsic desire, whereas my desire for money is instrumental, since I desire it as a means to other ends.

Now, if I have an intrinsic desire for x, then I cannot be mistaken about what x is in itself. If I am mistaken about this, then, strictly speaking, I do not desire x in virtue of what it is in itself; I desire x in virtue of what I *think* x is in itself. So, a desire theory that only counted the satisfaction of intrinsic desires would not need to adopt a rationality constraint. Let us apply this idea to the cases at hand.

Consider (1). Is it true that I have an intrinsic desire for drinking the orange liquid? No, my reason for drinking it is that I mistakenly think it will be tastier. My intrinsic desire is about drinking some-thing tasty. Since I believe that the orange liquid is tasty, I form an instrumental desire to drink this liquid, but satisfying this desire will not make me better off.

Consider (2). Again, my desire for treatment B is an instrumental desire formed on the basis of an intrinsic desire to stay alive and a belief that B will cure me, so, again, satisfying this instrumental desire will not make me better off.

Consider (3). A desire for a certain career path is plausibly seen as an instrumental desire. I have an intrinsic desire for a job with cer-tain general features: adventurous, multifaceted, dynamic, flexible, demanding, and so on. And I mistakenly think that a philosopher's job has all these features to a high degree. Choosing the career as a philosopher will therefore not make me better off.

Finally, consider (4). Again, my desire not to indulge myself too much seems to be an instrumental desire that is based on an intrinsic desire to avoid doing what God disapproves. So I would not satisfy my intrinsic desire by avoiding self-indulgence and, consequently, I would not be better off.

This shows, I think, that there is no need to impose a rationality constraint to deal with cases (1) to (4).

IDEAL DESIRES VERSUS ACTUAL DESIRES

But can we not imagine cases where the satisfaction of our *intrinsic* desires seems irrelevant to our well-being? Note that our intrinsic desires can be formed by means of social pressure, indoctrination, brain washing, and other manipulative methods. For example:

> [a] person who had a life of misfortune, with very little oppor-tunities, and rather little hope, may be more easily reconciled to deprivations than others reared in more fortunate and affluent circumstances [. . .] The hopeless beggar, the precarious landless labourer, the dominated housewife, the hardened unemployed or the overexhausted coolie may all take pleasures in small mercies.[10]

Do we really want to say that these unfortunate people, who have been forced to take great pleasures in small mercies, have good lives because they get exactly what they intrinsically want?

To avoid this implication, one could claim that we should only count *ideal* intrinsic desires, the intrinsic desire that we would have if we knew all relevant facts and reasoned rationally. If these unfortunate people knew how their intrinsic desires were formed, they would no longer hold these desires. For example, if the dominated housewife knew that she formed her intrinsic desire to please her husband just as a way of coping with the submissive role assigned to her by society, she would no longer hold this desire.

However, it is doubtful whether a rationality constraint of this kind is of any help. First, it is not impossible that the housewife would in fact endorse her desire to please even if she were to know about how it was formed. After all, if she is deeply convinced that she deserves no better life, this conviction need not be abandoned once all empirical facts about her desire to please are on the table. Of course, one could make the constraint stronger by demanding that ideal desires are those that one would have if one knew all relevant facts including the evaluative facts, such as the fact that one deserves a better life.

But this move will not deal with cases where the ideal self knows the evaluative facts but does not care much about them. For example, suppose that the dominated housewife would not care much about the fact that she deserves a better life. Indeed, we can suppose that she has already been told by close friends that she should not put up with her submissive role. Even if she acknowledges that this is true, she can still fail to be moved simply because of fatigue and apathy.

To deal with this, we could qualify ideal desires further and demand that they are the desires we would have if we had full knowledge about empirical and evaluative facts and were exclusively interested in what is objectively desirable. But then ideal desires become an idle wheel. A person's good is simply what is objectively desirable for the person. Since ideal desires are defined as tracking objective value, it is trivially true that something is good for a person only if it is endorsed by his ideal desires.

A more general worry with only counting ideal desires is that actual desires are completely ignored. I would certainly have been a very different person if I had known all empirical and evaluative facts concerning my actual desires. Suppose I want to drink cheap wine, play football, and listen to 50s Rock 'n' Roll. But perhaps I would not have had any of these desires, if I had been fully ideal and known all relevant evaluative facts. Does this show that it is not good for me to satisfy my actual desires? Why should we think that the desires of 'ideal-me' should decide what is good for 'actual-me' when our personalities and tastes can be so different?

I think that we should resist the move to ideal desires. Adaptive desires pose a serious problem, but, as I will explain later, there is another solution available that does not disregard actual desires.

COMMON PROBLEMS FOR SUBJECTIVE ACCOUNTS OF WELL-BEING

Malevolent pleasures and desires

We have seen that some of the defects we found in hedonism could to some extent be fixed by a desire theory. I will now turn to some general objections to both hedonism and desire theory.

The first objection concerns malevolent desires and pleasures. Is it good for an immoral person to have his immoral desires satisfied or to feel immoral pleasure? For instance, is it good for the sadist to have his sadistic desires satisfied and to feel sadistic pleasure? Is it good for the Ku Klux Klan-member (KKK-member) to satisfy his desire to lynch the black man and to feel pleasure in doing this?

In answering these questions, we need to make clear that we are talking about 'good for' in the sense of well-being. We can all agree that these satisfactions are not good for him *as a moral agent* – they do not promote his moral standing, and make him a better moral agent. But even if this confusion is avoided, is it sensible to count malevolent desires?

Note that the personal restriction does not rule out malevolent desires, for personal desires can also be malevolent. The sadist's fundamental desire/pleasure might be that *he* tortures the victim, and the devoted KKK-member, that *he* takes part in lynching the black man.

One way to sweeten the pill is to note that it is only by admitting that the immoral person has a life that is good for him that we can make sense of the common complaint that life is unfair. If the vicious people's pleasures and desire satisfactions did not make them better off, how could we consistently claim that it is unfair that they are better off than virtuous people?

The more serious problem is rather that once it has been granted that immoral pleasures and desire satisfactions are good for people, utilitarianism will have very grim implications. Here are two vivid illustrations of this problem (I will assume that maximizing overall desire satisfaction and maximizing overall pleasure coincide in the following cases):

(1) *Ethnic cleansing.* The majority ethnic group want to kill the minority ethnic group. The minority want to live. But if the majority is sufficiently large, then their desires should rule, and we have to say that what the majority does to the minority is morally right.

(2) *The Roman Circus.* The Romans in the audience want the victims to die a painful death. The victims want to survive. If we have sufficiently many in the audience, then their desires should rule, and we have to say that what the Romans are doing is morally right.

These grim implications follow, since utilitarianism is wedded to welfarism and maximizing act-consequentialism, which together imply that total well-being ought to be maximized.

The standard response is to agree that these actions are right, but that the examples are very far-fetched and our intuitions should therefore not be trusted. In real life, the options are almost never restricted to either satisfying or frustrating immoral desires. There is often a third option of *changing* these desires. So, the best choice is to get rid of malevolent desires and replace them with innocent desires and satisfy these. For instance, regarding the Roman Circus, Hare points out that, 'The right thing to have done from the utilitarian point of view would have been to have chariot races or football games or other less atrocious sports; modern experience shows that they can generate just as much excitement'.[11]

But what if the agents in question cannot rid themselves of the immoral desires? Assume, for instance, that the majority ethnic group harbours such a deep seated hatred towards the minority group that they have only two options: act on this hatred and kill the minority or not act on it. If they are sufficiently many, the majority should kill the minority. In fact, the stronger unalterable interest the majority takes in killing the minority, the better it is for them to kill the minority. So, the problem still stands.

Adaptive pleasures and desires: the Stoic Slogan

We have already noted that desire theory will have problems with adaptive desires. But the problem is more general. All subjective theories of well-being seem to be committed to the Stoic Slogan: If you cannot make the world conform to people's desires, you should make their desires conform to the world. Or, put in a formulation that is more relevant to hedonism, if you cannot make the world please people, change them so that they are pleased about the world.

What exactly is the problem with following the Stoic Slogan? Rawls complains that following the Stoic Slogan reduces us to bare persons who 'are ready to consider any new convictions and aims, and even abandon attachments and loyalties, when doing this promises a life with greater overall satisfaction'.[12] This means, he continues, that as a bare person you cannot lead a life 'expressive of character and of devotion to specific ends'.[13] This argument can of course be applied to cases where we can affect the well-being of other people. If I can turn someone else into a bare person, the Slogan, and, consequently, utilitarianism, seems to tell me that it is better to do so.

One reply to Rawls' complaint is to say that most of us are simply unable to become bare persons. Some desires of ours are so deeply seated that we cannot get rid of them. A more general reply is to say that even if we can become bare persons, it is not clear that giving up our deep commitments and projects will maximize desire satisfaction, for deep-seated desires are often held for a longer time and with stronger intensity than short-lived desires.

However, these replies do not go to the heart of the matter, for we can easily imagine more realistic cases where desire-adjustment seems problematic. Recall the examples about the unfortunate people who adjust to oppressive circumstances by taking pleasure in small mercies.

OBJECTIVE WELL-BEING THEORIES TO THE RESCUE?

At this point, one may think that the only remedy is to abandon the subjective account of well-being and go for an objectivist account, according to which what makes something good or bad for a person need not be a subjective feature of him. For we could then say that it is just bad for people to do immoral things or feel immoral pleasures, just bad for people to be deceived, just bad for people to put up with small mercies, and these things are bad for people no matter what they feel about them. Of course, a sensible objectivist can accept that some goods and bads depend on subjective features; it is just that they do not exhaust the list of all goods and bads.

To adopt an objective account of well-being would of course be a clear break from classical utilitarianism, but note that one could still stick to consequentialism and welfarism and thus remain a utilitarian. One could say that moral rightness depends exclusively on outcome-values and that these values, in turn, are in part determined by objective well-being.

However, I will show in the next section that there is still one move available to the utilitarian, a move that does not go so far as to say that some goods and bads are good or bad, no matter what the person feels about them. I will cash it out in terms of a desire theory, but attitudinal hedonism could be revised along similar lines.

HYBRID ACCOUNT

To find an acceptable solution, we need to get a bit clearer about what exactly makes adaptive desires so problematic. It cannot be the mere fact that the desires are adaptive. Often it is perfectly reasonable to adapt your desires to circumstances that cannot be changed. Suppose, for instance, that you desperately want to become a professional opera singer, but you simply do not have the voice for it. Suppose, further, that once you accept your limitations you abandon your opera ambitions and go for the more modest goal of singing in a local amateur choir. Why should it not be good for you to satisfy this more modest ambition?

Much more important is the fact that adaptive desires often do not seem to be about things that are *worthy of concern*. Satisfying desires that concern things that are not worthy of concern does not seem to make us (much) better off. For instance, a person whose main aim is to count the blades of grass on public lawns seems to have desires that are seriously misplaced. The strength of this desire does not seem to match the value of the desired object. I am not saying that there is no value in counting the blades of grass. Perhaps there is some excellence involved, endurance, for instance, so that the achievement merits an entry in the Guinness Book of World Records. But to make grass-counting the main aim is to care too much about something that has only minor value. Similarly, someone who takes great pleasure in small mercies seems to take an all too great an interest in something that is not worthy of great concern. Finally, what makes a bare person such an odd figure is not that he is willing to change his desires, but that he is willing to change his desires no matter whether his new desires will be for something more valuable. Replacing ones old aims and convictions with new ones is appropriate when the old aims and convictions were concerned with things of little or no value. Likewise, abandoning loyalties and attachments is perfectly accepta-ble when they concern people who are not worthy of our concern.

This diagnosis is not new. In fact, it seems that Mill had something similar in mind when he drew a distinction between higher and lower pleasures and claimed that it is better to be Socrates dissatisfied than a fool satisfied.[14] Socrates' higher pleasures, even if imperfectly real-ized, are on the whole more valuable than the fool's lower pleasures, because Socrates' pleasures concern things of higher quality such as great intellectual achievements.

If this diagnosis is right, it shows that it is not enough to adopt a rationality constraint. There is no guarantee that rational and informed desires will match up with worthwhile activities, for an informed and rational grass-counter or a bare person is not an impos-sibility. Nor does it help to count only autonomously formed desires. A bare person is surely autonomous if he freely adopts the Stoic Slogan and decides to live by it despite the objections raised by his family and friends.

What we need to do is to adopt a more discriminating desire theory. What makes a person better off is not simply that he gets what he would favour. It is also important that his favourings are about things that are worthy of concern. This is of course to reject desire theory in its purest form. But note that on the revised view, it is still true that nothing can be good for a person if it is not favoured by him. So, this theory is radically different from a pluralist theory that would accord value to worthwhile activities even if they were not endorsed.

At this point, some might object that my well-being theory is unstable. Once it is recognized that the objective value of achieve-ments matter to well-being, why not give some independent weight to excellent achievements? In reply, I would say that we have to dis-tinguish between the different kinds of value a life can possess. A life full of artistic or scientific achievements will have instrumental value for the society as a whole even if the person himself does not see the point of what he is doing and thus fails to endorse his life. This life can also have perfectionist value and be a good instance of its kind, a good artistic or scientific life, for instance. But I maintain that if he is cold and indifferent towards his life, it is not *good for him* even though it may be good for others, and a good artistic or scientific life. The discrepancy between what is worthwhile in his life and his attitudes explains what is so tragic about a depressed but successful achiever. He had it all in terms of objective value but was unable to appreciate it.

Of course, much more needs to be said before we have a complete theory of well-being. One major task is to give an account of the values that merit a positive response. It is of course important to exclude prudential values. We would get a circular account if we said that something is good for a person because he favours it and it is good for him.[15] What we are looking for are non-prudential values and excellences. There is no need to restrict the values to only one kind of excellence, such as moral virtue. That would give us an all too moralized conception of well-being. It is more promising to embrace the whole range of excellences and values, including moral, social, intellectual, aesthetic, and athletic ones.

It should be noted that, to a certain extent, these excellences and objective values are already taken into account by an ordinary desire theory, for, normally, we do not just want to do or be things, we want to do things *well* and be *good*. For instance, if you want to be a parent, you normally want to be a *good* parent.[16] It is strange to say, 'Yes, I want to be a parent, but I do not mind being a very bad one.' Similarly, if you want to be a friend, you want to be a *good* friend; if you want to be an athlete, you want to be a *good* athlete, and so on. Now, since your desire to be a good x can only be satisfied if you really are a good x, it is not enough that you believe that you are a great x, for you may be wrong.

What is important for my purposes here is that a value-sensitive desire theory is able to discriminate between favourings on the basis of their content and not just their strength. This means that transforming a person into a bare person or a grass-counter is not always the best option even if the person displaying either of these odd character traits would favour his life strongly. Allowing or making sure that a person develops into a normal person with normal aspirations is usually the better option, since then his favourings will be more in line with what is objectively valuable. I am not assuming that the lives of these odd characters must be bad for them and not worth living.

I am just saying that they will normally have lives that are less good than the lives of normal people.

More generally, the revised account takes the edge off the Stoic Slogan. Whereas the pure desire theory tells us that it is better to make our favourings conform to the world, the revised theory tells us, much more plausibly, that it is better to make our favourings conform to what is *worthwhile* or *valuable* in the world.

A final worry is that this stress on what is objectively worthwhile and valuable might seem to license a paternalistic approach to child rearing and education. One could imagine a nightmare scenario in which pushy parents spend all their time and energy to make sure that their children are exposed to 'high culture' from a very young age. Instead of relaxing and engaging in pleasant idle play with their children, the parents will be hot-housing their young ones by, if necessary, coercing them to read classic literature, go to museums, learn to play a musical instrument, and take ballet lessons.

This objection assumes that the objective values at stake only involve intellectually, aesthetically, or physically demanding activities. But nothing in the revised desire theory requires us to take such a narrow view on objective values. Some important values will be found in close intimate relationships which can only develop if enough time is set apart for spontaneous interaction.

Even if greater objective value is attached to the more demanding excellences, we need to remember that these objective values do not provide intrinsic benefits if they are not intrinsically endorsed. If our children pursue these values only because they want to please us or avoid negative sanctions, they are not appreciating these values for their own sakes. By hot-housing our children we might succeed in getting them to pursue valuable activities, but if they cannot see the point of these activities, they will not reap any intrinsic benefits from engaging in them.

This hybrid view seems to provide a pretty good solution to the problems that faced a purely subjective account of well-being. There is one problem remaining, however, which is that it is unclear whether this account can be combined with a consequentialist theory of moral rightness. The hybrid view claims that some favourings are to be discounted because they concern immoral activities. But can a consequentialist really accept this? It seems to lead to some kind of circularity: rightness and wrongness are determined by outcome-values, and these values are determined by well-being, but this in turn, is in part determined about what is moral or immoral, that is, right or wrong. So, it looks like on this account facts about rightness and wrongness will in part be determined by facts about rightness and wrongness. Is there a way out of this circle?

One way to avoid this circle would be to say that it is not the fact that certain desires are *immoral* that prevents them from having a positive impact on the well-being of a person; what prevents them is the fact that they are *malevolent*, that they concern things that are *bad for* other people. The clearest example of this is the sadist who takes pleasure in another person's suffering. The hybrid view could claim that suffering is bad for people, and that to desire or take pleasure in what is bad for people is not good for the sadist. There is no obvious circularity here.

CONCLUDING REMARKS

We have seen that the subjective conception of well-being, embraced by classical utilitarianism, is problematic in many respects. It does not give us an adequate theory of what well-being consists in. Nor does it provide us with a well-being candidate that we think we have moral reasons to promote in all cases. A better conception of well-being combines both subjective and objective features. The subjectivist is right to say that nothing can be good for a person unless he favours it, but we should add that how good something is for him depends crucially on how worthy of concern it is.

SUGGESTED READING

On the concept of well-being:

Feldman, F. (2004), *Pleasure and the Good Life*, Oxford: Oxford University Press, Chapter 1.

Griffin, J. (1990), *Well-Being: Its Meaning, Measurement, and Moral Importance*, Oxford: Clarendon Press, Part One.

Kagan, S. (1992), 'The limits of well-being', *Social Philosophy and Policy*, Vol. 9, No.2, 169–189.

Parfit, D. (1992), *Reasons and Persons*, Oxford: Clarendon Press, Appendix I.

Raz, J. (1986), 'Personal well-being', *The Morality of Freedom*, Oxford: Clarendon Press, Chapter 12.

Sumner, W. (1996), *Welfare, Happiness, and Ethics*, Oxford: Clarendon Press, Chapters 1–2.

On hedonism, general:

Bentham, J. (1823), *The Principles of Morals and Legislation*, London: T Payne (originally printed 1789), Chapters 1 and 3.
Crisp, R. (2006), *Reasons and the Good*, Oxford: Oxford University Press, Chapter 4.
Feldman, F. (2004), *Pleasure and the Good Life*, Oxford: Oxford University Press, Chapters 2, 3, and 8.
Mill, J. S. (1871), *Utilitarianism*, London: Longmans, Green, Reader & Dyer, Chapter 2.
Sumner, W. (1996), *Welfare, Happiness, and Ethics*, Oxford: Clarendon Press, Chapter 4.

On attitudinal hedonism:

Feldman, F. (2004), *Pleasure and the Good Life*, Oxford: Oxford University Press, Chapter 4.

On desire-based theory:

Brandt, R. (1979), *A Theory of the Good and the Right*, Oxford: Clarendon Press, Part I.
Brandt, R. (1996), *Facts, Values, and Morality*, Cambridge: Cambridge University Press, Chapter 2.
Gibbard, A. (1992), 'Interpersonal comparisons: preference, good, and the intrinsic reward of a life', in Elster, J. and Hylland, A., (eds.), *Foundations of Social Choice Theory*, Cambridge: Cambridge University Press, 165–193.
Griffin, J. (1990), *Well-Being: Its Meaning, Measurement, and Moral Importance*, Oxford: Clarendon Press, Chapters 1–2.
Harsanyi, J. (1982), 'Morality and the theory of rational behaviour', in Sen, A. and Williams, B., (eds.), *Utilitarianism and Beyond*, Cambridge: Cambridge University Press, 39–62.
Kraut, R. (1997), 'Desire and the human good', in Carson, T. and Moser, P., (eds.), *Morality and the Good Life*, Oxford: Oxford University Press, 164–176.
Rabinowicz, W. and Österberg, J. (1996), 'Value based on preferences: On two interpretations of preference utilitarianism', *Economics and Philosophy,* Vol. 12, 1–27.
Scanlon, T. (1975), 'Preference and urgency', *The Journal of Philosophy,* Vol. LXXII, No.19, 655–669.
Sen, A. (1985), 'Well-being, agency and freedom: The Dewey lectures 1984', *The Journal of Philosophy,* Vol. LXXXII, Section II, 169–221.

On the hybrid theory of well-being (or the endorsement theory, as it is now often called):

Bykvist, K. (2006), 'What are desires good for? Towards a coherent endorsement theory', *Ratio*, Vol. XIX, No 3, 286–304.

Darwall, S. (1999), 'Valuing activity', in Paul, E., Miller, F. and Paul, J., (eds.), *Human Flourishing*, Cambridge: Cambridge University Press, 176–196.

Dworkin, R. (2002), *Sovereign Virtue*, Cambridge, MA: Harvard University Press, Chapter 6.

Kraut, R. (1994), 'Desire and the human good', *Proceedings and Addresses of the American Philosophical Association*, Vol. 68, No. 2, 39–54.

Parfit, D. (1993), *Reasons and Persons*, Oxford: Oxford University Press, 493–502.

CHAPTER FIVE

UTILITARIAN AGGREGATION

The utilitarian wants to make the world a better place by making it a better place for people. Hence he judges the outcomes of his actions by how they affect people's well-being. This chapter deals with the way the utilitarian aggregates the well-being of different people when he determines the overall value of an outcome. I shall critically examine *sum-ranking*, the aggregation principle favoured by classical utilitarians. This principle has been accused of (1) caring about total well-being and not about individual well-being, (2) ignoring the distinction between persons, (3) treating persons as mere containers of well-being, and (4) disregarding inequality of well-being. I shall discuss whether these charges against utilitarianism are reasonable. I will also say something about whether well-being can be measured in the way that is required for sum-ranking to work.

SUM-RANKING

Recall the core aggregation principle of utilitarianism:

Sum-ranking
One outcome is better than another if and only if it contains a greater total sum of well-being.

Recall also that the sum of well-being is calculated in the following way, again assuming hedonism for the sake of simplicity. Take an individual who exists in the outcome. Go through all his pleasures and assign a positive value to each according to how intense the pleasure is. The higher the intensity, the higher is the positive value assigned. Sum these values. Go through all his displeasures and assign a negative value to each according to how intense the displeasure is. The higher the intensity, the lower is the negative value assigned.

Then sum the pleasure values and the displeasure values, and we will get the person's lifetime value. Repeat this procedure for all individuals in the outcome. Finally, sum all the individuals' lifetime values. This is the total sum of well-being contained in the outcome.

UTILITARIANS CARE TOO LITTLE ABOUT THE WELL-BEING OF INDIVIDUAL PEOPLE

One common complaint against a utilitarian who is committed to sum-ranking is that he seems to care only about total well-being and not the well-being of individual people. It is true, of course, that the utilitarian is not completely ignoring the well-being of individuals, since total well-being is made up of the well-being contributions of individuals. But these contributions seem to matter only in so far as they make up total well-being. It is still true to say that what matters fundamentally is total well-being, since this is what we ought in the end to maximize.

However, this objection assumes a straw man. Any sensible utilitarian would say that each individual's well-being matters fundamentally in the sense that it has value in itself. It is precisely this fact that explains why total well-being has intrinsic value, for this total is nothing but a whole consisting of intrinsically valuable parts. Total well-being has no intrinsic value except in virtue of containing these intrinsically valuable parts.

UTILITARIANS DO NOT TAKE SERIOUSLY THE DISTINCTION BETWEEN PERSONS

However, this reply will hardly satisfy the critic. Even if it is granted that the well-being of each individual matters in the sense that it has intrinsic value, individual well-being does not seem to matter in the right way, since the utilitarian must be prepared to sacrifice one person's good for the sake of other people's goods. What is wrong with sum-ranking is not so much that it assigns value to the wrong things; it is rather that the things assigned value are so easily interchangeable. According to Rawls, the problem

is the consequence of extending to society the principle of choice for one man, and then, to make this extension work, conflating all persons into one [. . .].[1]

A similar view is expressed by Thomas Nagel, who complains:

[utilitarianism] ignores the distinction between persons [. . .] To sacrifice one individual's happiness for another's is very different from sacrificing one gratification for another within a *single* life.[2]

The problem is that utilitarianism draws a false analogy between the aggregation of well-being within a single person's life and the aggregation of well-being across different persons' lives. That this analogy cannot be too close is obvious. It seems to be conceptually confused to say that *your* suffering is compensated for by *my* happiness. For whom would this be a compensation? Not you, because you never received a benefit. Not me, since I did not suffer in the first place. It only makes sense to talk about compensations within a single life, as when my painful visit to the dentist is compensated for by the pleasure of my having functioning teeth.

Now, it is clear that the utilitarian is not guilty of such an obvious confusion, for he can say that one person's gain outweighs another person's loss without saying that there is someone whose loss is compensated for by the gain. To say that my gain outweighs your loss is just to say that the value of my gain is greater than the disvalue of your loss, and that, as a consequence, the outcome where I gain and you lose is overall better than the outcome in which I lose and you gain.

Some utilitarians seem to accept a deeper analogy between trade-offs within a life and trade-offs between lives. In Chapter Three, we saw that one could understand utilitarianism as a sort of generalized self-concern. On this model, an ideal moral agent identifies with other people and imaginatively puts herself in their shoes. You can approximate this ideal by asking how you would feel about being in the other person's situation. If you succeed in this identification, you will view things from his perspective and the objects of his desires will present themselves as attractive to you. Once you have 'taken over' the desires of others you proceed in the normal way and perform the action that will give you the greatest overall satisfaction of desires. In this way, conflicts of desires of different people are transformed to conflicts of desires within a single agent. In particular, on this model, one person's weak desire can be outweighed by another person's strong desire, since, when they are imaginatively taken over by the agent, it is rational for him to act on his strongest desire.

It is true then that this objection has some force if utilitarianism is understood as generalized self-concern. But recall that there is an alternative understanding of utilitarianism, one according to which the ideal agent is seen as an impartial and benevolent judge. On this model, the fact that one person's gain can outweigh another's loss is just a consequence of an impartial and benevolent evaluation of gains and losses. From a wholly impartial benevolent perspective, it cannot matter *who* is experiencing a loss or a benefit. In Mill's words, 'equal amounts of happiness are equally desirable, whether felt by the same or by different persons'.[3] So, if my gain in well-being is greater than your loss, it seems that impartial benevolence dictates that the size difference is the only thing that matters, and that therefore my gain should be seen as outweighing your loss.

Of course, even if this impartial model of utilitarianism does not 'conflate all persons into one', one could still question its plausibility. One could, for instance, question its plausibility because one simply rejects any trade-offs between different people.

No trade-off
We are never justified in making one person worse off in order to make other people better off.

But this principle is absurd. Any reasonable moral theory must accept some trade-offs between people. The most important moral problems are about balancing gains and losses of different people. Surely, we are allowed to make one person slightly worse off in order to prevent some horrible suffering for a lot of other people.

So, classical utilitarians need not conflate all persons into one. They are just giving an answer to the important question of how one should weigh one person's gains against another person's losses. Of course, you may not be happy with this answer. But what you should say then is that utilitarianism is wrong because it gives us the wrong trade-off principle, not that it is wrong because it gives us a trade-off principle in the first place.

What is it then that is so problematic about the utilitarian trade-off principle? Well, one serious problem is that utilitarianism must accept *unrestricted* trade-offs between people.

Unrestricted trade-off
Any loss, no matter how great, to some people can be justified by
making sufficiently many other people only slightly better off.

To give you a vivid illustration of this implication, suppose that a workman is stuck in the machinery in the transmitter room of a television
station. If we leave him there, he will suffer excruciating pain. If we
help the workman, the transmission of a football match will be interrupted and millions of viewers will be slightly disappointed.[4] Unrestricted trade-off says that it is better to let the workman suffer the
excruciating pain, even though the benefits to each viewer are minor.

This particular example also shows that utilitarianism does not
seem to give proper weight to *suffering*. One person's suffering, no
matter how severe, can always be outweighed by a sufficiently large
number of very small benefits to other people.

Note that it does not help here to say that malevolent pleasures or
desire satisfactions should be discounted, for the viewers are not
malevolent; they only take a mild interest in an innocent football
match. Disregarding malevolent pleasures would only take care of
the cases where a lot of people take a mild sadistic interest in the
severe suffering of one unlucky person.

What can the utilitarian do then? One option is simply to bite
the bullet and insist that small benefits, if sufficiently numerous, can
outweigh great losses and severe sufferings. To make this more palat-
able, the utilitarian could point out that this is what we implicitly
accept in many real cases anyway. For example, we think it is justified
to build a bridge in order to make it more convenient to travel between
two places, even when we know that some workmen will die or be
severely injured during the construction of the bridge. But the benefit
to each traveller – the convenience of saving some time – seems small
in comparison to the loss to the workmen – death or severe injury.

Another way to make unrestricted trade-offs more acceptable is
to say that our intuitions about these cases are not to be trusted since
we have in general a hard time grasping big numbers. For instance,
as John Broome points out, 'many people's intuition tells them that
the process of natural selection, however many billions of years it
continued for, could not lead from primordial slime to creatures with
intelligence and consciousness. But they are wrong. Four billion years
will do it'.[5] In analogy, Broome suggests we may also have a hard

time imagining the vast number of very small benefits that would be needed to outweigh a very severe harm.

No doubt, these hard-nosed responses will not convince everyone, not even people who have strong utilitarian tendencies. Is there no way to make the utilitarian theory more attractive?

One option is to revise utilitarianism so that it only takes into account suffering. Sum-ranking is then replaced by

Negative utilitarianism
One outcome is better than another if and only if it contains a *smaller* sum of total *suffering*.

But this move is not recommended. First, it does not take care of the transmitter room case because we can suppose that each viewer will experience some discomfort when the match is interrupted. But if we add up a sufficiently large number of these small discomforts, the total sum of suffering will be greater than the suffering experienced by the single workman.

This assumes, of course, that small discomforts count as a form of suffering, and that can be challenged. But suppose instead that the viewers are all devoted football fans and would truly suffer for a short time if they missed the match – this is the match of their lives! Given a sufficiently large number of devoted fans, negative utilitarianism would still think it is better to let the workman suffer excruciating pain for months. So, not even negative utilitarianism seems to give the right weight to suffering.

A second and pretty obvious reason to reject negative utilitarianism is that it does not give any weight at all to positive well-being. This implies that nothing can be better than an 'empty' world in which no creatures experience any well-being. It also implies that there can never be any trade-offs between suffering and positive well-being, not even if the suffering is short and the positive well-being immense and long-lived. But that is absurd. Surely, a few minutes of suffering for one person can be compensated for by extending the lives of billions of other people, making sure that they all have fantastic lives.

UTILITARIANS TREAT PERSONS AS RECEPTACLES OF WELL-BEING

So far, we have been considering cases where the population is fixed. In these *same people cases*, as they are often called, we can only affect the well-being of people but not the number and identity of people. But there are many real-life choices that do affect both the number and the identity of people, such as abortion, use of contraception, and large scale population policies. Let us now see how utilitarianism deals with these *different people* cases.

In this new context, sum-ranking would imply that there are two ways of adding goodness to the world: Either you *prolong* a happy life or you *create* a new happy life. Consequently, a utilitarian who embraces sum-ranking cannot distinguish between these two ways of bettering the world, if the extra amount of happiness would be the same in both cases. But this seems to suggest that the utilitarian treats people as *receptacles* for well-being. Compare: If you have a number of buckets of water and want to get more water, you can either pour more water into the buckets you already have or get a new bucket and fill it up. The utilitarian seems to treat people as buckets and well-being as something to be poured into these buckets.

This complaint resembles the one discussed earlier – that utilitarians do not care about individual well-being. However, on this new version of the objection, it is conceded that the utilitarian cares about the well-being of individuals and not just total well-being. The complaint is rather that the utilitarian cares about individual well-being only because he cares about well-being for its own sake and not because he cares about people for their own sake. Since well-being cannot be free-floating, it needs a receptacle, a person. But it is only in this derivative sense that the utilitarian cares about people. Compare: The wine connoisseur cares about the wine for its own sake, but cares only derivatively about the wine bottles, since he knows he cannot store the wine without pouring it into bottles.

Again, the metaphors used are not fair to utilitarianism. Remember that the utilitarian cares about what is good for individual persons. Indeed, he cares about it so much that he assigns intrinsic value to each person's well-being. This is one important way to care about persons. If you are indifferent to how well or badly off someone is, you cannot be said to care about the person. If I care about you, I do things for your sake, but that seems to imply that I also care about your well-being. What motivates the utilitarian to be indifferent between prolonging happy lives and creating happy lives is that he cares *equally* about *everyone's* well-being, including the well-being of people whose existence is contingent on his actions. As Sidgwick pointed out, for the impartial utilitarian 'the good of any one individual is of no more importance, from the point of view (if I may say so) of the Universe, than that of any other person'.[6]

Even if the utilitarian cannot be seen as treating people as mere receptacles for well-being, it is still true that they must be indifferent between prolonging a happy life or creating a happy life, if the extra amount of happiness would be the same in both cases, but this is counter-intuitive. Should we really be indifferent between prolonging a life with, say, 35 years of positive well-being and creating a new person, who will live for 35 years at the same level of positive well-being? Isn't it more important to make people happy than to make happy people? For future reference, let us call this 'the problem of replaceability'.

Another problematic implication of utilitarianism for different people situations is that any decrease in the level of individual well-being can be counterbalanced by an increase in the number of people enjoying this lower level of well-being. But this means that the utilitarian must say that a population in which everyone's life is very good is worse than a much bigger population in which everyone's life is just above the level at which life is worth living. For instance, the utilitarian must think it is better to encourage people to create a huge number of children, even if theirs and their children's lives will be only barely worth living, than to encourage them to have fewer but extremely happy children. This implication is illustrated more schematically in Figure 5.1.

In this figure, the width of each block shows the number of people, and the height shows how much above the neutral level these lives are. The A-people have lives that are way above the level at which

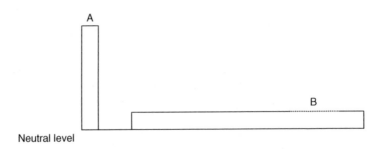

Neutral level

Figure 5.1

a life is worth living, whereas the B-people have lives that are barely worth living. What is a life that is barely worth living? It may be a life that has enough ecstasies to make its agonies seem just worth enduring or it may be of uniformly poor quality. Imagine being asleep most of the time, or as Derek Parfit suggests, a life full of 'muzak and potatoes'.

Since B's area is greater than A's, the total sum of well-being in B must be greater than that in A, and thus the B-population must be judged better than the A-population. For many, this is clearly the wrong result, and it has even been dubbed '*the repugnant conclusion*' by Parfit.[7]

It might be tempting to think that the problem of replaceability and the repugnant conclusion can be avoided if we aggregate well-being by taking the average rather than the total sum of well-being.

Average-ranking
One outcome is better than another if and only if it contains a greater *average* of individual well-being.

Average-ranking will say that it is better to make an existing person better off than to create an additional well-off person, for making an already existing person better off will always yield a higher average (as long as the extra amount of well-being for the new person and that for the already existing person would be the same). It will also avoid the repugnant conclusion since the average well-being is much lower in the B-population.

Unfortunately, average utilitarianism has a clearly unacceptable implication: you can make things better by creating horrible lives, full of unspeakable suffering. Consider a population of truly horrible lives. If we add to this population a person with a slightly less horrible life, we will raise the average. So, according to average utilitarianism, this is an improvement!

Another response to the problem of replaceability and the repugnant conclusion is to say that classical utilitarianism goes astray because it is too impersonal. We should care about individual well-being, but only in the sense that we should care about whether people are *better off* or *worse off*. More exactly, the restriction could be stated thus,

Person-affecting restriction
An outcome A is better than another B only if someone is better off in A than in B.

An outcome A is worse than another B only if someone is worse off in A than in B.

To decide whether a person is better off in one outcome than in another we need to compare how he would fare in the respective outcomes. If his level of well-being in one outcome is higher than his level of well-being in another outcome, then he is better off in the first outcome. This implies that creating a new person cannot make him better off than he would otherwise have been, for *he* would not have been at all, if he had not been created. A person can have a level of well-being in an outcome only if he exists in that outcome.

If the utilitarian accepts the person-affecting restriction, he can avoid both the replaceability problem and the repugnant conclusion. It is not better that a happy person is replaced by an equally new happy person, since by creating a new happy life we are not making anyone better off than he would have been; we are only making it worse for the already existing person by not prolonging her life. It is not better with a huge population with lives barely worth living than a smaller one with perfect well-being, since the extra people in the huge population are not better off having lives barely worth living than not having any lives at all.

So far so good. But this restriction is not reasonable. It does not allow that we can make an outcome worse by creating people with short and excruciatingly painful lives, for, creating these persons does not make them worse off than they would otherwise have been. If you cannot make a person better off by creating her, then neither can you make a person worse off by creating her. So, it is too drastic to say that what matters are only facts about who is better off and worse off. We do also care about the creation of new lives and whether they will be good or bad for the people who live these lives. Would anyone deny that creating a population with horrible lives is worse than creating a completely different population with perfectly happy lives, just because we cannot say that any particular person is better off in the happy population than in the unhappy population?

However, it is hard to accept that making new happy people is as good as making existing people happy. So, the right approach is perhaps to give some weight to making happy people but more weight to making people happy. In any case, it is important to note that these problems are not unique to utilitarianism. They are problems for any reasonable moral theory that takes the well-being of individuals seriously. Any plausible moral theory has to have something to say about choices that affect the number and identity of people, and what it says must be sensitive to how these choices determine who will exist and how well or badly off they will be. The literature on these problems – population ethics, as it is now often called – shows that it is very difficult, if not impossible, to find an intuitively attractive solution. But this is perhaps not so surprising after all, since our standard principles of beneficence were formulated, first and foremost, to take care of *same people cases* where the identities of people are fixed. It is an unfortunate fact that when these principles are generalized to different people cases they often have unpalatable consequences. To avoid these extra complexities, I will put different people cases aside in the rest of the book.

EQUALITY AND PRIORITY

So far we have been discussing objections to utilitarianism that centre on the idea that utilitarianism does not care in the right way about persons and their well-being. A different complaint is that it cares too little about *relations* between different people. More specifically, it does not give any weight to the distribution of well-being between people. So, in a choice between distribution A and distribution B in Table 5.1 below, no weight is given to the fact that in A there is great inequality and in B perfect equality.

It is important to make clear that the objection is about the distribution of well-being, not the distribution of well-being *sources*. A utilitarian could accept that it is often better to equalize well-being sources by, for instance, taxing the rich and giving the money to the poor, for the simple reason that the loss in well-being for the rich is

Table 5.1

	Distribution A	Distribution B
My well-being	19	10
Your well-being	1	10
Total well-being	20	20

normally smaller than the gain in well-being for the poor. Typically, the poorer you are, the more an extra pound matters to your well-being. Conversely, the richer you are, the less a lost pound matters to your well-being.

A radically revised form of utilitarianism could claim that inequality is bad because it is bad in itself for you to be worse off than others. The idea is not that you are worse off because you envy the people that are better off, or that the better off people treat you with pity so that you lose self-respect. The idea is much more radical than that. It is that the mere fact that someone is better off than you makes you worse off, no matter whether you know or care about this inequality. Obviously, this idea is not an option for classical utilitarians, since they have to say that you cannot be worse off without this affecting your subjective states.

But is it really a sensible option? Would we accept that we are worse off by the fact that somewhere in the universe there is some population of aliens that are much better off than we are, even though we have no idea about their existence and well-being levels?

If this move is resisted, the utilitarian seems forced to accept that inequality is not intrinsically bad after all. Of course, they can still claim that inequality of well-being is *instrumentally* bad in the sense that general knowledge about such inequality tends to generate unpleasant and undesired consequences for the worse off, such as envy and loss of self-respect. But is this enough?

At this point, the classical utilitarian could turn the tables and say that it is in fact not sensible to assign intrinsic disvalue to inequality, for if you do, you have to accept that you can make the world better in one respect without making anyone better off. Indeed, you have to accept that you can make the world better in one respect even though you make *everyone* worse off. To see this, consider this schematic example in Table 5.2.

Table 5.2

	Distribution A	Distribution B
My well-being	19	−10
Your well-being	1	−10

If you are an egalitarian and think that inequality is intrinsically bad, you have to say that B is better than A in one respect (no inequality) even though everyone is worse off in B (indeed, we are both suffering in B).

This 'levelling down' objection, as it is has been dubbed, seems to have some force. In fact, it ties in nicely with the person-affecting view of morality we discussed earlier, according to which what matters fundamentally is how people are affected. On this view, equalizing well-being cannot be regarded as an improvement if it does not make anyone better off.

But did we not discredit the person-affecting restriction? Yes and no. We did discredit it as a restriction to be applied to different people cases. But it seems much more plausible to apply it in same people cases.[8]

So, the 'mind the gap' approach that assigns intrinsic disvalue to inequality seems to come with significant costs. However, there are other ways to take into the distribution of well-being. One way is to give priority to the worst off people. The crucial question is then 'How much?' An extreme answer is that all weight is given to the worst off. This is often called *Maximin* (which is short for *Maxi*mizing the *Min*imum):

Maximin
One distribution is better than another if and only if the worst off in the first distribution are better off than the worst off in the second distribution.

Maximin is clearly unacceptable, however, since the slightest increase in the well-being of the worst off will outweigh any loss, no matter how great for the better off. For instance, in the case set out in Table 5.3, B must be judged as better than A.

Table 5.3

	Distribution A	**Distribution B**
My well-being	30	1.00000000000001
Your well-being	1	1.00000000000001

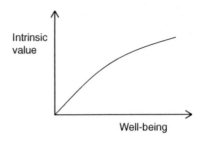

Figure 5.2

A better way of giving priority to the worst off is to say that each person's well-being is given some weight, but more weight is given to the well-being of worse off people. More exactly, the idea is that the weight depends on the person's *absolute* level of well-being, so the weight assigned to your well-being level does not depend on the well-being levels of other people. However, the lower the absolute level of well-being, the more weight is assigned to that level of well-being. We can illustrate this with the graph in Figure 5.2.

The values on the vertical axis represent the intrinsic values of lives, and the values on the horizontal axis, the absolute well-being levels of these lives. That the graph slopes upward shows that all benefits count. That it bends downward shows that less weight is given to a benefit if it is received by someone with higher well-being. The resulting theory, *prioritarianism* as it is now often called, could then be stated thus.

Prioritarianism
One distribution A is better than another if and only if the sum of all the weighted well-being levels in A is higher than the corresponding sum in B.

Note that prioritarianism, in contrast to egalitarianism, does not assign any intrinsic value to relations between people; it only assigns intrinsic value to individual lives.

Prioritarianism will avoid the problems with maximin, since the losses for better off people will always count for something even though they count for less than the losses for worse off people. It will also take care of the levelling down objection, since, on this view, things get worse if everyone is made worse off. Prioritarianism seems to fare better than standard utilitarianism in problematic trade-off cases, such as the TV transmitter case. Since the absolute level of well-being of the suffering workman is lower than the absolute level of well-being of the disappointed football fans, the workman's loss in well-being would be given more weight than the gain in well-being for the football fans. This means that we need many more disappointed fans to outweigh the severe suffering of the single workman. Of course, there will always be a sufficiently large number of football fans whose total well-being gain will be greater in value than the great loss in well-being for the workman. But if much more weight is given to people with a low level of well-being, we would need so many fans that it is no longer realistic that this kind of case could occur on earth.

Enemies of unrestricted trade-off would of course complain that it is still possible to *imagine* a scenario where we do have the sufficient number of small benefits, and insist that this is enough to discredit prioritarianism, since it would give the intuitively wrong result for this possible but far-fetched situation.

A popular reply to this complaint is to say that we should not put much confidence into our intuitions about far-fetched possibilities. Our moral intuitions are more reliable for situations that are closer to actuality, since it is in this environment they have been formed in the first place.

So, should utilitarians happily embrace prioritarianism? One problem with prioritarianism is that, on the face of it, it does not seem to square with impartiality, one of the cornerstones of utilitarianism. If I give more weight to worse off people, I seem to be biased in favour of some people over others, and that does not look like impartiality. Compare: if I give more weight to the well-being of the rich and famous, I seem to be show bias towards some people over others.[9]

However, it is not clear that this is a good objection. Strictly speaking, it is not true that prioritarianism favours worse off people over better off people. Prioritarianism is only concerned with the absolute well-being levels of individuals; it is not concerned with whether people are better or worse of than others. So, how the value of a life does not depend on how it fares in comparison to other lives; it only depends on the absolute well-being level of the life. I can be better off than you in one situation, and worse off than you in another, but if my absolute level stays the same in both situations, its weight will also be the same. Furthermore, prioritarianism does give exactly equal weight to benefits that are received by people at the same absolute level of well-being. (It should also be noted that giving more weight to the rich and famous violates another utilitarian principle, namely, welfarism, since being rich and famous is not good in itself for people.)

Another, more pressing, problem for prioritarianism is that it is not clear how the weights should be determined. Exactly how much weight should we give to a person at a certain absolute well-being level? If the different weights given to the worse off and the better off differ only marginally, then the resulting theory will come pretty close to classical utilitarianism. If they differ radically, then too little weight is given to the better off.

MEASURING WELL-BEING

Throughout the discussion in this chapter we have simply assumed that it makes good sense to compare the well-being of different individuals. We have assumed that we can meaningfully say that one person is better off than another person but also, more controversially, that one person's gain is greater than another's loss. In fact, in order to apply sum-ranking we even need to be able to say *how much* greater a certain gain is compared to another loss. But is it true that we can quantify well-being in this precise manner?

Now, no one seriously doubts that we can say that one person is better off than another. Would anyone deny that the destitute leper who is dying on the streets of a slum is worse off than a healthy and happy person in an affluent society? What people doubt is to what extent we can make sense of comparisons of gains and losses in the well-being of different people. It is important to note that how problematic this is depends crucially on what is supposed to be the constituents of well-being. Consider a wildly implausible theory of well-being that says that the well-being of a person simply consists in his girth. Rounder people are better off than thinner ones, and how much better off they are given by how much rounder they are. This theory does not have any problems comparing one person's gain to another person's loss (but that is of course its only virtue).

The more serious problems of comparisons of well-being across people arise when degrees of well-being are supposed to correspond to the degrees of qualities that do not readily allow for comparisons across people. Subjective conceptions of well-being seem to fare particularly badly in this respect. Whereas we think it is normally fine for you to compare the intensities of your pleasures – after all, the intensities of your pleasures are just a matter of how things feel to you – it seems more questionable to compare your pleasure gains with my pleasure losses. Even though your pleasure gains feel a certain way to you and my pleasure losses a certain way to me, there is no one to whom both your pleasure gains and my pleasure losses feel certain ways. Similarly, it seems fine to say that your preference for coffee over tea is weaker than your preference for life over death, since this more or less amounts to saying that you would not be willing to sacrifice your life in order to have a cup of coffee even if the alternative would be a life which only offered tea. But it seems much more problematic to say that my preference for coffee over tea is weaker than your preference for life over death, since, again, there is no one to ask whether he would be willing to sacrifice his life for coffee. If you ask me, you will only get an answer that enables us to compare *my* preference for coffee over tea to *my* preference for life over death. If we ask you, we will only get information about how *your* preference for coffee over tea compares to *your* preference for life over death.

These are formidable problems, no doubt, but they have to be put in perspective. First of all, no one denies that we can make *some* comparisons of changes in subjective states of different people. For instance, the pain increase I feel when my dentists starts to pull out all my teeth without anaesthetics is certainly greater than the pain increase you feel when someone gives you a pin prick. Similarly, my preference for staying alive is typically stronger than your preference for scratching your nose. The question is not so much whether we can make these comparisons, but how to explain this possibility.

There is an enormous literature on this topic and many different views have been defended. There is no space to discuss them here. What is more important to note is that any plausible moral theory will have to face the problem of comparisons of subjective states across people. The reason is simple. Since any plausible moral theory has to take into account well-being, any plausible theory has to take a stand on what constitutes well-being. Obviously, if one goes for a subjective account, one has to face the problem head on. But the same holds for plausible objective accounts. To get into trouble about comparisons it is enough to give *some* weight to subjective factors when comparing the well-being of different people. For instance, even if knowledge and friendship are good for you, no matter how you feel about these things, there is surely a difference in well-being between, on the one hand, someone who has worthwhile knowledge and good friends and also takes great pleasure in these things, and, on the other hand, someone who has knowledge and friends but, because of chronic depression, is unable to take much pleasure in these worthwhile things. But this innocent-looking evaluation assumes that it makes sense to compare 'not much pleasure' for one person to 'great pleasure' for another. Furthermore, we need to compare my loss of well-being with your gain in well-being when I become depressed and lose some but not all interest in knowledge and friends and you come out from your depression and regain an interest in having knowledge and friends. So, the problem of well-being comparisons is everyone's problem. It is just that for the utilitarians it is such an obvious and pressing problem, since for them subjective well-being is the only thing that matters for moral rightness.

It should be stressed, however, that although utilitarians need to make comparisons of well-being differences across people, they do not need to assume that these differences can be compared with great precision. A utilitarian could accept that the comparisons are often indeterminate. So, for instance, he could accept that even if it is clear that my gain is greater than your loss, it might be indeterminate exactly how much greater my gain is. Perhaps all we can say is that my gain is at least twice but not more than three times greater than your loss. These rough comparisons can be fed into the utilitarian evaluations with the result that sometimes two outcomes are incomparable in value: one outcome is neither better than, worse than, nor equally as good as the other.

Note, however, that indeterminate well-being comparisons of this kind are still compatible with some determinate outcome evaluations. For instance, suppose that we know that my gain is at least twice but not more than three times greater than your loss. Suppose, further that your sister's loss is less than yours, but it is indeterminate how much less. Then the result is still that my gain is guaranteed to outweigh you and your sister's losses taken together, since it is universally true that a (my gain) must be greater than $b + c$ (you and your sister's losses taken together), if a is at least twice but not more than three times as great as b, and c is smaller than b. However, we cannot say that my gain outweighs your loss and three exactly similar losses to your three cousins, since it is not universally true that a must be greater than $3 \times b$, if a is twice as great but not more than three times as great as b.

Of course, if these 'gappy' outcome evaluations are combined with maximizing consequentialism, we will get a lot of normative gaps as well. When some available outcomes are incomparable there will be no right (permissible) actions, since a right action has to have an outcome that is comparable to the outcome of *any* alternative action; more specifically, it has to be at least as good as that of any alternative action. To avoid this paralyzing result, we could revise the standard definition of rightness and say that an action is right if and only if its outcome is *not worse than* the outcome of any alternative action. To see how this works, suppose that the action A's outcome is better than B's and C's, but that A's outcome is incomparable to D's outcome. If these are all the alternatives, we can still say that A is right because its outcome is not worse than that of any of the alternative actions, B, C, and D.

In the rest of this book, I will simply assume that we can quantify well-being in the strong sense required by sum-ranking. This idealization simplifies the discussion and makes it easier to see exactly what utilitarianism says about various cases. The question of how to be a utilitarian in a situation with poorer quantitative well-being information, pressing though it certainly is, falls outside the present work.

CONCLUDING REMARKS

We have seen that sum-ranking has many unattractive consequences. But the utilitarian is not stuck with them. There are many alternative methods of aggregation available to a non-classical utilitarian. However, as we have also seen, it is not easy to spell out in detail how a plausible alternative would look like. The alternatives we have considered – negative utilitarianism, average utilitarianism, the person-affecting restriction, egalitarianism, and prioritarianism – are all problematic in certain respects, (prioritarianism less so than the others). They are also much more complicated than the simple and clean sum-ranking idea. So, the crucial question is whether what we lose in simplicity by abandoning sum-ranking is compensated for by what we gain in intuitive attractiveness by accepting a more complex aggregation method.

It should be noted that the question about aggregation cannot be brushed aside by non-utilitarians, for any plausible moral theory must provide some guidance on how to aggregate different people's well-being.

SUGGESTED READING

On utilitarian aggregation:

Broome, J. (1995), *Weighing Goods: Equality, Uncertainty and Time,* Oxford: Wiley-Blackwell, Chapters 4 and 10.

On the separateness of persons objection:

Brink, D. (1993), 'The separateness of persons, distributive norms, and moral theory', in Frey, R. G. and Morris, C. W., (eds.), *Value, Welfare, and Morality*, New York: Cambridge University Press, 252–289.

Nagel, T. (1970), *The Possibility of Altruism*, Oxford: Oxford University Press, 138.

Nozick, R. (1974), *Anarchy, State, and Utopia*, New York: Basic Books, 31–34.

Rawls, J. (1972), *A Theory of Justice*, Oxford: Oxford University Press.

On negative utilitarianism and the weight of suffering:

Mayerfeld, J. (1999), *Suffering and Moral Responsibility*, New York: Oxford University Press, Chapter 6.

Popper, K. (1962), *The Open Society and its Enemies*, Vols. 1 and 2, London: Routledge, Vol. 1, 284–285 and Vol. 2, 387.

Smart, R. N. (1958), 'Negative utilitarianism', *Mind*, Vol. 67, 542–543.

On the person-affecting restriction:

Arrhenius, G. (2009), 'Can the person-affecting restriction solve the problems in population ethics?', in Roberts, M. and Wasserman, D, (eds.), *Harming Future People. Ethics, Genetics and the Nonidentity Problem*, Dordrecht, Netherlands: Springer, 289–314.

Parfit, D. (1993), *Reasons and Persons*, Oxford: Oxford University Press, Part 4, Chapter 16, Section 125.

Temkin, L. (1993), 'Harmful goods, harmless bads', in Frey R. G. and Morris C. W., (eds.), *Value, Welfare, and Morality*, New York: Cambridge University Press, 291–324.

On egalitarianism:

Broome, J. (1995), *Weighing Goods: Equality, Uncertainty and Time*, Oxford: Wiley-Blackwell, Chapter 9.

Temkin, L. (1993), *Inequality*, New York: Oxford University Press.

On prioritarianism:

Holtug, N. (2006), 'Prioritarianism', in Holtug, N. and Lippert-Rasmussen, K., (eds.), *Egalitarianism. New Essays on the Nature and Value of Equality*, Oxford: Oxford University Press, 125–156.

Parfit, D. (1997), 'Equality and priority', *Ratio*, Vol. 10, No. 3, 202–221.

On population ethics:

Arrhenius, G. *Population Ethics. A Challenge For Moral Theory* (under review by Oxford University Press).

Broome, J. (2004), *Weighing Lives,* Oxford: Oxford University Press.

Parfit, D. (1993), *Reasons and Persons*, Oxford: Oxford University Press, Part 4.

On measuring well-being:

Broome, J. (2004), *Weighing Lives,* Oxford: Oxford University Press, Chapter 5.

Hammond, P. J. (1991), 'Interpersonal comparisons of utility: Why and how they are and should be made', in Elster J. and Roemer J. E., (eds.), *Interpersonal Comparisons of Well-Being*, Cambridge: Cambridge University Press, 200–254.

CHAPTER SIX

A USER-FRIENDLY GUIDE TO ACTION?

Utilitarianism is a simple and powerful theory. It tells you to follow the same principle in all possible situations, namely, 'Maximize total well-being'. On the face of it, then, it does not seem to be difficult to apply it in a particular case. You just need to find the option that will bring about the highest total amount of well-being. Since there is only one principle to follow, there is no need to look out for conflicts between different principles and, when they do conflict, figure out how to weigh them against each other.

But appearances are deceptive, because it is in fact very difficult to use utilitarianism as a direct guide to action. For one thing, you need to know how your actions will affect the well-being of people in the distant future; for another, you seem to be required to care only about well-being, care equally about everyone's well-being, and, as a consequence, care as much about the well-being of total strangers as the well-being of your nearest and dearest. But these requirements seem to go beyond our normal expectations of moral agents. That his theory is not user-friendly should worry the utilitarian, for isn't a normative theory supposed to guide action? Indeed, isn't that one of the main purposes of a normative theory?

In this chapter I will critically examine the accusation that utilitarianism is not user-friendly and see what the utilitarians can say in their defence. I shall start by discussing the knowledge problem for utilitarianism – that we often cannot know what we ought to do – and then move on to discuss the motivational problems.

WE CANNOT KNOW WHAT WE OUGHT TO DO

In a trivial sense, utilitarianism is easy to apply. Whenever you have a belief about which of your alternatives will maximize total well-being, you can also form a belief about what you ought to do. But the problem is rather that it seems difficult, if not impossible, to apply the theory *correctly* and do what utilitarianism in fact prescribes for the situation at hand.

According to utilitarianism, knowledge of our actions' immediate impact on well-being is not sufficient to decide what is right, since the distant future might hide some nasty surprises. Burying radioactive waste in the ground might seem like an excellent idea if you only consider the immediate effects this will have on people, but things look very different if you start thinking about the effects this will have on future generations.

The utilitarian must take the knowledge problem seriously, but before we consider possible utilitarian responses, it is important to put this problem in perspective, since, as we shall see, adopting a non-utilitarian theory does not take us out of the woods.

(a) The importance of future suffering

Any reasonable moral theory must contain some principle of beneficence or non-malevolence, saying that it is prima facie wrong to cause future suffering. But to know whether your action will cause future suffering, you might have to look into the distant future – some suffering might occur hundreds of years from now. Think again of the consequences of burying dangerous atomic waste in the ground. So, any reasonable moral theory that pays attention to future suffering will have to tackle the problem of knowing the future. Of course, the problem is especially noticeable for utilitarians, since they think that facts about present and future well-being are the only facts that are morally relevant. However, it is important to be aware that, even if principles of non-malevolence are put aside, non-utilitarian theories do not make it much easier for us to know what we ought to do, as the following points make clear.

(b) Unclear and vague crucial terms

Some deontological principles contain terms so vague and unclear that you cannot tell what you ought to do. For instance, some claim that you should not intentionally kill innocent persons, except in certain extreme situations. But they often give no clear guidance on how to understand 'intention', 'killing', 'innocent', 'persons', and 'extreme situations'. For instance, is intentionally allowing someone to die an instance of killing? Is late abortion a killing of a person? Is self-defence an extreme situation that justifies killing? If so, what exactly is self-defence? Is a situation in which I can save fifty people by killing one innocent person so extreme that I am justified in killing the innocent? If not, what about a situation in which we have a billion lives at stake? If this does qualify as an extreme case, then we need to decide where the cut-off point lies between saving fifty and saving a billion. But how do we decide this?

Unless deontological theories provide answers to these pressing questions, we cannot apply them universally, and thus we cannot know what we ought to do in many important situations. Utilitarians, in contrast, do not need to answer these questions, since in order to know how to maximize total well-being we do not need to know the exact meaning of 'intentional killing', 'innocent person', and 'extreme situation'.

(c) Weighing prima facie duties

Many deontological theories provide a list of different *prima facie* duties. Some are positive, for instance, a duty to help people in need and a duty to take care of your own children. Some are negative, for instance, a duty not to lie, a duty not to kill, and a duty not to harm. To have a prima facie duty does not mean that you ought, all things considered, to do something. Rather, your overall obligation is supposed to be determined by weighing the various prima facie duties. But here deontological theories often have very little to say. They often do not provide clear trade-off principles. For instance, is the duty not to break promises more stringent than the duty not to cause minor physical harm? If there is no clear answer, you cannot know what you ought to do, all things considered, in many cases.

Utilitarians, however, do not need to weigh different prima facie duties, since they think there is only one overall duty, namely, to maximize total well-being. Of course, utilitarians have an analogous problem when it comes to the aggregation of individual well-being: they need to know whether one person's gain outweighs another person's loss. But, as I have already argued, this seems to be everyone's problem, since no plausible moral theory can turn a blind eye to the question of how to weigh benefits against harms.

(d) Exceptions

Some deontological theories avoid this talk about weighing, maintaining instead that moral principles have implicit exception clauses: 'It is wrong to kill except in circumstances . . .', 'It is wrong to lie except in circumstances . . .'. But all too often these clauses are not spelled out. And that means, of course, that, again, we will not know what we overall ought to do in many cases. Again, this is not a problem for utilitarians, since there are no exceptions to the overall duty to maximize total well-being.

(e) Knowledge about the past

Utilitarianism is a forward-looking moral theory, since what you should do depends on the future consequences of your actions. In contrast, many deontological theories are backward looking. They tell you to keep past promises, to compensate for past wrongdoings, to give people what they deserve based on what happened to them in the past or what they did in the past. Therefore, knowledge about which action fulfils a duty requires knowledge about the past, but this might not be that easy to come by. For example, Robert Nozick defends an idea about distributive justice according to which a distribution is fair and ought to be maintained if it resulted from a chain of fair transactions, stretching into the past and ending at a point where someone justly appropriated some unowned material resources.[1] Now, some of these transactions might have taken place way back in the past, and hence it might be virtually impossible for us now to know if all the transactions in the chain were fair. Suppose, for instance, that you wonder if the land you inherited from your parents is rightly owned by you. To decide this, you need to find out whether the first settlers appropriated the land in a just manner, and, further, whether they passed the property on in a just manner, and, even further, whether each such transaction, leading up to your present ownership, was fair. This is surely a daunting task.

(f) Knowledge about your own psychological make-up

For many deontologists, the psychological make-up of the agent matters a great deal for the moral rightness of his action. For instance, whether an effect is intended or only foreseen matters a great deal for rightness, according to the double-effect doctrine. You are permitted to do good, knowing and foreseeing that this will cause something bad, but you are not permitted to do something bad in order to do good. But this means that if I want to know whether your action is permissible, it is not enough for me to look at the effects of your actions, as the utilitarian would do; I need to know what you intended and what you only foresaw. But it is often extremely difficult to know the exact nature of another person's intentions and beliefs, especially when the person would not give you a truthful answer, if asked. Indeed, the person might not be fully aware of his own intentions and beliefs and thus be unable to give you a truthful answer. But this means that not even the agent himself can always know whether his actions are permissible. A doctor can, for instance, be confident that he is administering a painful drug to a patient just because he wants to cure the patient, when in fact he does it partly because he takes pleasure in the mild suffering of an annoying patient.

Virtue theories will have similar problems, if they claim that the right action is the one that expresses a virtuous motive of the agent. The famous rock star who helps starving children might think he is acting on purely benevolent motives when in fact he is mainly after some social credit that will help his record sales. This lack of self-knowledge need not be easy to overcome.

Some Kantian theories will of course be in a similar position, since to know whether an action is right, according to these theories, you need to know whether the fundamental maxim you are acting on could be rationally willed to become a universal law. But, as Kant himself acknowledged, it is not always transparent to us which maxim we are acting on.

Again, utilitarianism will avoid these problems, since the agent's intentions will not have any bearing on the rightness of his actions. If you come across a drowning child who could only be saved by you, it is right for you to save the child, no matter whether your intention is to do the right thing, to be benevolent, or just to impress his mother.

(g) Knowledge about external features of the action other than its effects

Kantian theories will not just have problems with lack of self-knowledge. Even if you know which maxim you are acting on, you may not know whether your maxim could rationally be willed to become a universal law, because you have no clear views about what it is rational to will. Furthermore, even if you happen to be an expert on rational willing, you also need to know what would happen if the maxim were to become a law, and whether the resulting situation would be logically or conceptually coherent. But this requires good imaginative and logical powers, which we cannot expect to find in all moral agents.

A virtue theory that does not judge actions by the virtuous motives of the agent can avoid the problem of self-knowledge. On this theory, an action is right just in case it would be performed by a fully virtuous person. So, an action can be right even if it is performed by an agent who is not virtuous; it is enough that the action *would* have been performed by a fully virtuous person. This theory will instead have problems with knowing what a fully virtuous person would do. This seems to require knowledge about which character traits are virtuous and how they come together to form the unified character of a fully virtuous person. Again, this knowledge is not easy to come by.

What these examples show is that the knowledge problem is far from unique to utilitarianism. Only very simple-minded and obviously false moral theories can easily be used in the sense that you can always easily find out what you ought to do and then act on this knowledge. For instance, a theory that tells you to do what you feel like doing is easy to use but obviously false.

This is not to say that the knowledge problem is not a real problem for utilitarianism. Nor is it to say that utilitarians are in a better position to solve it. The deontologists could argue that it is much more difficult to gain knowledge about the future consequences of our actions than it is to gain knowledge about our own minds or the past behaviour of others. But this advantage does not count for much, if they also accept a prima facie duty to prevent future suffering, for then the knowledge problem is compounded.

TWO RESPONSES

There are two general responses to the knowledge problem available to the utilitarian.

(1) Blame us, not the theory

The most hard-nosed response is to accept that most of the time we simply have no clue about what we ought to do. But this is a failing in us rather than in utilitarianism. A moral theory, such as utilitarianism, is supposed to give an account of what makes an action right, but we should not expect it to be easy to apply the theory in real life. In this sense, moral theories are similar to other explanatory theories. For instance, no one would fault a theory of physics if it turned out that normal people could not apply it in real life.

On this view, the only thing we can do in response to the knowledge problem is to raise human capacities to the level where humans can more easily apply the theory, perhaps by employing computers to enhance our informational and computational capacities. We should not tinker with the moral theory merely to disguise our own shortcomings.

This response is too radical, I think. It is true that a moral theory should provide an adequate explanation of what makes actions right, but, as I pointed out in Chapter Two, it has also a practical function; it is supposed to provide some guidance in moral deliberation.

(2) Blame the theory, not us

We should lower the ambitions of the moral theory to a level where fallible humans can meet them, for, as Frankena once said, 'Morality is made for man, not man for morality.'[2] But exactly how user-friendly should the theory be? Since some humans are more fallible than others, and our fallibility varies with circumstances, it is not clear how to define the right level of usability.

Of course, we can all agree that a moral theory should at least be able to guide *ideal* agents, who know all relevant empirical facts and can reason flawlessly. Moral theories that give us inconsistent prescriptions will even fail this minimal requirement. But this does not seem enough. Shouldn't a normative theory also guide less than fully ideal agents?

One obvious way to make utilitarianism easier to apply is reformulate it in subjective terms:

Subjective utilitarianism
An action is right if and only if the agent *believes* that it will maximize total well-being.

This theory is definitely much easier to apply – we only need to know what we happen to *believe* will maximize total well-being, not what in fact will maximize total well-being. But this subjective approach comes with considerable costs. Subjective utilitarianism will sanction the actions of people who have bizarre beliefs about what will maximize well-being. If a mentally ill person thinks that Satan will torment every human being if he does not shoot down all the people in a shopping centre, he ought to shoot down these people.

Also, even if we somehow restrict the theory so that it only applies to normal people, we will run into problems, for it is often not true that we have flat-out beliefs about what will maximize total well-being. For example, in situations of uncertainty, where we think that each action has many possible outcomes, some more likely than others, there is no action whose outcome we are certain about. Subjective utilitarianism would then say that there is no action that is right, just because we do not believe of any action that it will maximize well-being. But this is counter-intuitive. There seem to be right choices to be made in cases of uncertainty. Suppose, for instance, that you are approaching a blind intersection in the country, and that you are not certain that you will avoid a serious accident if you speed through the intersection without slowing down. Isn't the right decision then to be cautious and slow down?

To deal with this last problem, we could try to reformulate utilitarianism in terms of subjective *probabilities*:

Probabilistic subjective utilitarianism
An action is right if and only if it maximizes subjective expected total well-being.

We calculate the subjective expected total well-being in the following way. (1) List the possible outcomes of an action; (2) For each possible outcome, ask yourself how probable you think it is that the action will have that outcome (i.e., how strongly you believe that the action will have that outcome); (3) For each outcome, multiply the subjective probability of the outcome with the value you think it has in terms of total well-being; (4) Sum these products and you have the subjective expected total well-being of the action; (5) Repeat this procedure for all alternative actions. Probabilistic subjective utilitarianism now tells you to choose the action that has the highest subjective expected total well-being.

This theory will give us prescriptions in cases of uncertainty. For instance, suppose you are approaching the blind intersection and your beliefs about the probabilities and total well-being of the available outcomes can be summarized as shown in Tables 6.1 and 6.2. The subjective expected total well-being of your actions can then be summarized as shown in Table 6.3. Since the subjective expected value of slowing down is higher than that of speeding, you ought to slow down.

The probabilistic version of subjective utilitarianism will strike many as still too subjective, since rightness is based on the agent's own probability assessments and her own assessments of well-being. What if the agent's probabilities assessments are seriously misinformed? Suppose that a doctor prescribes a certain medicine for a minor skin complaint in the belief that it will be an effective and harmless cure. His belief is not well grounded; he only has a hunch that this is the

Table 6.1

	Possible outcomes	
	No serious accident	**Serious accident**
Slow down	Probability 0.99	Probability 0.01
Speed through	Probability 0.5	Probability 0.5

Table 6.2

	Possible outcomes	
	No serious accident	**Serious accident**
Slow down	Well-being 10	Well-being −100
Speed through	Well-being 20	Well-being −100

Table 6.3

	No serious accident	**Serious accident**	**Expected total value**
Slow down	0.99×10	0.01×-100	$9.9 + (-1) = 8.9$
Speed through	0.5×20	0.5×-100	$10 + (-50) = -40$

right medicine. Now, if all evidence available to him suggests that the medicine will very likely have only harmful effects – all the facts about the medicine are there in a book on his desk – would we still want to say that it is right for the doctor to prescribe the medicine?

The obvious option is to reformulate the utilitarianism so that it takes into account the *epistemic* probabilities of the agent, roughly, the probabilities he has good reason to assign to the outcomes of his options. This will take care of the sloppy doctor, for even if he did not in fact assign a high probability to the outcome that the medicine will have harmful effects, he still had good reason to do so.

It is important to note that the subjective and the epistemic approaches are available not only to utilitarians but also to non-utilitarians. In the face of the knowledge problem, non-utilitarians can make similar moves. They can choose to formulate their theories in subjective terms with the result that virtue ethics now says that an action is right if the agent believes that a virtuous person would do it, and Kantianism says that an action is right if the agent believes that it is based on a universalizable maxim. But this subjective move is not recommendable to the non-utilitarians either, since then their theories would condone the behaviour of mentally ill people and radically misinformed people. It is better to formulate the theories in epistemic terms. Virtue ethics would then say that an action is right if the agent has good reason to believe that the action would be performed by a virtuous person, and Kantianism, that an action is right if the agent has good reason to think that it is based on a uni-versalizable maxim.

OBJECTIVIST REPLIES

Should we then go for the epistemic formulation of utilitarianism? It is true that it seems superior to both the objective and the subjec-tive accounts because of its more intuitive prescriptions. But remem-ber that the original problem was to find a more user-friendly theory, one that makes it easier for us to find out what we ought to do. On this score, the epistemic account is definitely inferior to the subjective accounts, since it is much easier to find out what you in fact believe (and how strongly you hold these beliefs) than what you should believe. Furthermore, even if you do know your epistemic probabili-ties, the calculations of expected value need not be as easy as in the example above with the car driver. Your decision might involve many alternative actions, each with a host of possible outcomes. A correct calculation of expected value will then require both time and good arithmetic skills. So, the problem of knowing what we ought to do remains.

The objectivist could also point out that it is doubtful whether the epistemic account provides a more intuitive moral theory. Remember that an epistemic account is providing an alternative *explanation* of why an action is right, one according to which the right-making features will in part be epistemic in nature. So, on this theory, it is never true that facts about people's well-being will explain why an action is right. What explains why an action is right has to do with what the agent has reason to think about his impact on people's well-being. Not even in a case where you know that an action will harm a person is it true to say that it is the fact that the action will harm him that makes it wrong for you to perform the action.

This complaint can be applied more generally to non-utilitarian epistemic accounts. Think about Oedipus, who killed his father and made love to his mother. Judging by our common-sense views on patricide and incest, he seems to have acted wrongly on both counts. But what makes the story so tragic is that he did wrong even though he tried his best in the light of available evidence to avoid doing these wrongs.[3]

HAVE THE OBJECTIVE OUGHT AND EAT IT TOO. THE DISTINCTION BETWEEN OBJECTIVE AND SUBJECTIVE RIGHTNESS

Since each side seems to have a compelling case to make, perhaps both sides are right. Perhaps 'right' is ambiguous between 'objective rightness' and 'subjective rightness'. What makes an action objectively right is the fact that it maximizes total well-being, but what makes an action subjectively right is the fact that it maximizes expected total well-being. So, Oedipus did the objectively wrong thing but the subjectively right thing, whereas the car driver who sped through the intersection and was lucky did the objectively right thing but the subjectively wrong thing.

By disambiguating rightness we seem to be able to have the objective ought and eat it too. Things are not so rosy, however, since we still need to know which notion of rightness is more important. If we claim that they are equally important, we seem to face a moral conflict in the cases above, since what is objectively right is not what is subjectively right. It is also not a useful answer to our moral query about what we ought to do to be told that objectively you ought to do this and subjectively you ought to do something else. We want to know what we ought to do, *full stop*. We thus need to make up our mind about which notion is more important.[4]

A PROBLEM CASE FOR OBJECTIVISM

One possible line open to the objectivist is to say that the most important notion for the assessments of acts is objective rightness. Subjective rightness is instead important when it comes to the assessment of agents. When an agent lacks knowledge about what he ought to do but acts on the best evidence available, he is doing what is subjectively right. He is thus not to be blamed if it turns out that his action did in fact not maximize total well-being. After all, he has a good excuse since he was trying to do his best.

Unfortunately, this reasoning cannot always be successfully applied, as the following example shows. Suppose a doctor must decide on the correct treatment for a patient who has a serious skin complaint. Careful consideration of the literature has led him to the following options. B will relieve the condition but will not completely cure it. One of A and C will completely cure the skin condition; the other will kill the patient, but there is no way he can tell which of the two is the perfect cure and which is the killer.[5] To make the structure of the case clearer, let us put it the diagrammatical form of Table 6.4 (where it is made explicit that the agent's evidence divides equally between the two possible states of nature S1 and S2).

Table 6.4

Actions	States of nature	
	S1 (p = 0.5)	S2 (p = 0.5)
A	Complete cure	Death
B	Partial cure	Partial cure
C	Death	Complete cure

The intuitively right option is B even though this is guaranteed to be suboptimal in terms of the patient's well-being. The objectivist, however, must say that the right option is either A or C, (assuming that what is actually best for the patient is also what has the highest total well-being). But both A and C seems wrong since, for each action, the possible gain of performing it does not seem to compensate for the possible loss. To perform either action seems reckless.

The important point with this example is that the objectivist cannot say that, even though the agent would act wrongly in doing B, he does not deserve blame. He cannot say that because in this particular example the agent *knew* at the time that doing B would be suboptimal in terms of the patient's well-being and thus wrong, according to an objectivist theory. The objectivist cannot therefore claim that the agent is blameless because he acted in good faith. It is therefore unclear how the agent could avoid blame. How can a conscientious moral agent do wrong deliberately and knowingly?[6]

An epistemic account will not have this problem since it would say that B is right because it maximizes *expected* total well-being. To see this, assume that the well-being values are as depicted in Table 6.5.

The expected value of A is then $(0.5 \times 10) + (0.5 \times -100) = -45$, the same for C, and the expected value of A is $0.5 \times 6 + 0.5 \times 6 = 6$, which is therefore the right action.

One response available to the objectivist is to deny that a conscientious agent can never do wrong knowingly. This response starts with the observation that a morally conscientious utilitarian agent is someone who cares about the values of outcomes. As a rational agent, he should therefore be sensitive to the risk of bringing about something really bad. Now, if he does A or C he knows that he might be lucky and end up bringing about the best outcome for his patient.

Table 6.5

Actions	States of nature	
	S1 (p = 0.5)	**S2 (p = 0.5)**
A	10	−100
B	6	6
C	−100	10

But, he also knows that he might be unlucky and do a serious wrong by bringing about something that is really bad for his patient, namely, his death. How much should he care to avoid bringing about something really bad and how much should he care about avoiding doing wrong? Well, one thing is clear; he should not just care about avoiding doing wrong, for then he would do A or C, since each of these actions gives some chance of acting rightly, whereas B is doomed to be wrong no matter what happens. It seems more sensible to say that it is rational for him in this case to do a minor wrong, B, in order to avoid risking doing something really bad.

I will not try to settle this dispute here. It is more important to note that there seems to be a tension between the two functions we expect a moral theory to serve. On the one hand, we expect it to fulfil a theoretical function: to give an intuitively attractive criterion of what makes an action right or wrong. The epistemic account seems worse in this respect than the objective account. On the other hand, we want to use the theory as a guide to action. In this respect, subjective accounts are clearly superior to both the objective and the epistemic accounts. The epistemic account is perhaps slightly better in this respect than the objective account. It all depends on how difficult it is to know your epistemic probabilities and calculate the expected values of your actions.

A tentative conclusion is that the better a utilitarian theory fulfils its theoretical function, the worse it fulfils its practical function, and the more difficult it will be to know what one ought to do. This conclusion can of course be generalized to non-utilitarian theories as well, so we should not blame utilitarianism for being stuck in this dilemma.

WE CANNOT BE MOTIVATED TO DO WHAT
WE OUGHT TO DO

To apply a moral theory requires both knowledge of morally relevant facts and motivation to follow the prescriptions of the theory. So far we have only discussed the required knowledge. Another complaint against utilitarianism focuses on the required motivation and states that, even if we have all the required knowledge, utilitarianism is still not user-friendly because we cannot motivate ourselves to follow it.

A simple version of this objection would say that utilitarianism requires us to be impartial and care equally about everyone's well-being, but this is not something ordinary humans can do. We are psychologically hard-wired to be partial towards ourselves, our friends, and our family.

This objection fails, for two reasons. First, it is not true that utilitarianism says that we ought to be fully impartial and benevolent, if this is understood as having a certain attitude or feeling. Utilitarianism simply says that we ought to perform the *action* that would maximize total well-being. So, it tells us how we ought to act, not how we ought to feel. It is true of course that if we maximize total well-being we will in fact do what a fully impartial and benevolent agent would do – this, we have seen, is one way of presenting the attractiveness of the theory – but this does not mean that in order to do the right thing we must be fully impartial and benevolent. The rightness of an action depends only on the impact it has on total well-being, and not on the motivation behind the action. As Mill explained, 'He who saves a fellow creature from drowning does what is morally right, whether his motive be duty, or the hope of being paid for his trouble.'[7] If you save the drowning person just because you want to be rewarded, you are obviously not a fully impartial and benevolent person, but your action is still right if it maximizes total well-being.

Second, the objection assumes that we cannot be fully impartial and benevolent. But then utilitarianism would not even tell us to *become* fully impartial and benevolent, for 'ought' entails 'can', that is, if you ought to do something, it must be possible for you to do it. (Remember that utilitarianism tells you to do the best you *can* do.) Nor would utilitarianism tell us to *try* to become fully impartial and benevolent for most of us would just bungle it if we tried to become utilitarian saints. It is better to aim lower and succeed than to aim higher and fail. Indeed, as Sidgwick explained, 'if experience show that the general happiness will be more satisfactorily attained if men frequently act from *other* motives than pure universal philanthropy, it is obvious that these other motives are reasonably to be preferred on Utilitarian principles' (my italics).[8]

A better version of this objection would instead say that utilitarianism would sometimes require great sacrifice – you ought to throw yourself at the hand grenade to save your friends, for instance, but it is very difficult for us to be motivated to sacrifice our lives for the common good. This objection is not based on a misunderstanding of utilitarianism; it is true that utilitarianism will sometimes ask you to sacrifice your own life.

But, again, we have to be careful in spelling out this objection. If in a particular situation you cannot sacrifice your life, because you cannot motivate yourself to do it, then utilitarianism will not say that you ought to sacrifice your life, for it respects the principle 'Ought' entails 'Can'. Of course, we can still imagine cases where you can motivate yourself to make a significant sacrifice for others and you would succeed if you tried. Suppose, for instance, that you can muster the motivation to throw yourself at the hand grenade in order to save your friends and that you would succeed if you tried. Utilitarianism would then say that you ought to do it and that may seem all too demanding. Sacrificing your life is obviously a morally good thing, but it seems to go beyond the call of duty. I will come back to this objection in the next chapter.

UTILITARIANISM CONDEMNS ITSELF AS A GUIDE TO ACTION

If you use a moral theory as a guide to action, you apply it to your actions and act on the basis of its prescriptions. You avoid doing what it tells you is wrong, and you do what it tells you is obligatory. So, for instance, if you use utilitarianism as a guide to action, you calculate the (expected) well-being values of your options, compare these values, and choose the option that has the highest value. But since using a theory is itself an action that can have significant consequences, utilitarianism might in fact tell you not to apply it. For instance, it is clear that when you have the chance to save someone from drowning you will normally not have the *time* to go through a complete utilitarian calculation. If you do, the person will drown and it will be too late for you to do anything. Or think about situations in which good consequences will come about only if you act spontaneously. Acting, painting, and other artistic endeavours come to mind, but intimate conversations between friends are also good examples. Now, if you start thinking about the consequences of being spontaneous and deliberately decide to be spontaneous, you have blown it and your spontaneity is lost. Examples like these therefore show that *utilitarianism will sometimes condemn itself as a guide to action.*

Is this an unacceptable feature of utilitarianism? Well, remember that utilitarianism, first of all, provides a criterion of rightness. It tells us what makes an action right or wrong. This is not the same thing as providing a method of deliberation or a decision method which tells you how to deliberate. As hinted at in Chapter Two, this distinction is not special to moral theories. You can find it in all goal-directed activities. Basically, it is a distinction between aims and the means to the aims. Now, quite often a criterion of rightness, when applied, will be, as Sidgwick put it, 'practically self-limiting; *i.e* that a rational method of attaining the end at which it aims requires that we should to some extent put it out of sight and not directly aim at it'.[9] Here are some helpful examples, (the first of which is a repeat from Chapter Two).

Love. You want to find someone to love. This is your aim. However, if you constantly think about this aim and calculate whether the person in front of you is a good candidate then you will not find love. You will be sending such strange vibes that people will run away from you. The best method of deliberation is not to calculate in this way but to just enjoy the company of your date and focus on the conversation or the activity you are engaged in.

Tennis. You want to win. This is your aim. However, if you always think about it, you will not be sufficiently focused on the game and you will lose. The best method of decision is to concentrate on the game, for instance, by following Björn Borg's rule of thumb: Try to hit the ball 10 cm inside the line.

Egoism. You want to maximize your own happiness. This is your aim. However, if this is your aim, you will not succeed in maximizing your own happiness, for if you keep treating others as mere means to your ends, they will eventually notice it and then not treat you as a true friend. Instead, in order to maximize your own happiness, you have to take a genuine interest in what other people are doing, perhaps even take an interest in other people and not just treat them as mere means to your own happiness.

The distinction between a criterion of rightness and a decision method applies to many non-utilitarian moral theories as well. For instance, it is popular among virtue ethicists to claim that virtue is its own reward in the sense that acting on virtuous motives is good for us. Some also go further and claim that it is this very fact about our own flourishing that explains why acting on virtuous motives is morally right for us. Now, this feature of virtue ethics makes for problems when it comes to its action-guiding function, for if the agent were to be motivated to do the right thing because he correctly thinks that this will benefit him, he would not act virtuously. To be motivated to act by the thought that the act will benefit him, in the sense of making him a better human being, is to be morally self-indulgent and that is a vice. Instead, the agent should act on unselfish motives such as honesty, benevolence, and a sense of justice.

This shows that utilitarianism and some forms of virtue ethics share a drawback: they will sometimes tell agents not to be moved by the reasons that explain why an action is right. In the case of utilitarianism, it will tell an agent not to be motivated to promote overall goodness in all cases, because acting on this motivation will not promote overall goodness. Virtue ethics will tell the agent not to be motivated to pursue his own flourishing, because acting on this motivation is to display moral self-indulgence which is a vice. Both theories will therefore be self-effacing in the sense that it is not always right to act from what the theory itself says is the right reason.

In one respect, the problem seems more serious for virtue ethics, for it is *necessarily* self-effacing; it is impossible to act from the right reason and also act rightly. The problem for the utilitarian is a contingent one, since it is not impossible to act from a benevolent motive and succeed in maximizing total well-being.[10]

However, utilitarianism will not just condemn itself as a decision method. Unlike virtue ethics, it might also claim *that most people ought not even adopt it as a criterion of rightness.* Why is that? Well, the idea is that in many cases, if a person adopts utilitarianism and tries to follow it, he will produce a lot of unhappiness. Perhaps he will usually make mistakes and miscalculate when he tries to promote happiness. Or perhaps the person will fall victim to self-deception and rationalize personal interest under a utilitarian guise. A case in point: During the Vietnam War, some US military leaders adopted what they called 'utilitarian calculation' when they deliberated about how to fight the war. I do not think it is too wild to guess that these calculations were often skewed in favour of American lives.

In a choice between converting a person to utilitarianism or letting him stick to his old common sense, it might thus be best according to utilitarianism to let him stick to his old rules. This might mean that one should actively avoid promulgating utilitarianism publicly. If this is true, then utilitarianism condemns its own public promulgation. Is this a problem? Some people think it is. They think that any acceptable moral theory should meet a *condition of publicity*. It must be possible under any circumstances for us to accept a theory and promulgate it publicly without thereby violating that theory itself.

This is a questionable condition, however, since it means more or less 'let the theory be accepted and publicly promulgated, though the heavens fall'. Why should the utilitarian not be allowed to apply his theory to the public promulgation of the theory when this can have such drastic effects? To think otherwise seems question-begging, since, as Peter Railton points out, 'it would require that one class of acts – acts of adopting or promulgating an ethical theory – *not* be assessed in terms of their consequences'.[11]

Note, however, that utilitarianism might even imply that *no one* should believe it. Suppose, for instance, that there is an anti-utilitarian demon out there that will cause horrendous suffering any time anyone accepts and applies the utilitarian doctrine. In this extreme situation, no one should accept and apply utilitarianism. And if you happen to be a utilitarian you should as a soon as possible try to rid yourself of this idea. This sounds self-defeating. But wait a minute. If you really accept the distinction between a criterion of rightness and a decision method, why should this example bother us? If you are a utilitarian in this sad situation, you believe that you should stop believing it. But this reason is provided by the very criterion of rightness you accept. Of course, not only utilitarians can find themselves in this situation, since any plausible moral theory must have a disaster prevention clause. If the stakes are high enough, which they surely will be if we imagine a sufficiently vicious demon, we ought to stop believing the true morality.

CONCLUDING REMARKS

One bitter lesson from this chapter is that utilitarians might have to live with the fact that their theory is not so user-friendly. In particular, they might have to accept that we are often not in a position to know what we ought to do. However, this is a predicament they share with all decent non-utilitarians, since they too will have to accept that it is not easy to know what we ought to do. Only obviously flawed moral theories can be easily applied by all agents in all cases.

Utilitarianism fails to be user-friendly in another sense too: it sometimes condemns itself as guide to action. But, again, this is a problem that is shared by non-utilitarian theories as well, for example some popular forms of virtue ethics. So perhaps, no matter which morality you adopt, thinking in moral terms may prevent you from acting morally.

SUGGESTED READING

On the knowledge problem:

Jackson, F. (1991), 'Decision-theoretic consequentialism and the nearest and dearest objection', *Ethics*, Vol. 101, 461–482.

Oddie, G. and Menzies, P. (1992), 'An objectivist guide to subjective value', *Ethics*, Vol. 102, No. 3, 512–533.

Smith, M. (2006), 'Moore on the right, the good, and uncertainty', in Horgan, T. and Timmons, M., (eds.), *Metaethics after Moore*, Oxford: Oxford University Press, 133–148.

Zimmerman, M. (2008), *Living with Uncertainty. The Moral Significance of Ignorance*, Cambridge: Cambridge University Press.

On the distinction between criterion of rightness and decision method:

Bales, R. E. (1971), 'Act utilitarianism: Account of right-making characteristics or decision making procedure', *American Philosophical Quarterly*, Vol. 8, 257–265.

Bergström L. (1996), 'Reflections on consequentialism', *Theoria*, Vol. LXII, Part 1–2.

Sidgwick, H. (1907), *The Methods of Ethics*, seventh edition, London: Macmillan, 78, 119, 121.

Tännsjö, T. (1995), 'In defence of theory in ethics', *Canadian Journal of Philosophy*, Vol. 25, No. 4, 571–594.

On subjective and objective oughts:

Gibbard, A. (1990), *Wise Choices and Apt Feelings*, Cambridge, MA: Harvard University Press, 42–43.

Sidgwick, H. (1907), *The Methods of Ethics*, seventh edition, London: Macmillan, 207–209.

Zimmerman, M. (2008), *Living with Uncertainty*, New York: Cambridge University Press, 7–8.

On self-effacing moral theories:

Parfit, D. (1993), *Reasons and Persons*, Oxford: Oxford University Press, Part 1.

Railton, P. (1984), 'Alienation, consequentialism, and the demands of morality', *Philosophy and Public Affairs*, Vol. 13, No. 2, 134–171.

CHAPTER SEVEN

IS UTILITARIANISM TOO DEMANDING?

It is clear that since for the utilitarian only the best is good enough, there is no room for doing less good than you can. If you fail to do what is best in terms of total well-being, you are simply doing wrong. But maximizing total well-being can be very demanding, as the following illustrations show.

HEROISM

After you have saved a child from a burning building you are told that there is another child still left in the building. You could go back into the building and save the second child, but you know that this will cause you third-degree burns. According to utilitarianism, this would not just be a heroic thing to do; you *ought* to do it, and it is wrong not to do it.

YOUR MONEY AND CHARITY

You are wondering whether to spend a pound on chocolate for yourself or to give it to a certain charity. You know that this charity is unusually effective and that even a small contribution can help them save a child from some crippling and painful illness. Since you obviously do more good by saving a child from illness than by eating a piece of chocolate, you ought to give the pound to charity. However, if you repeat this utilitarian reasoning every time you have a pound to spare, you will end up very poor indeed.

EVERYDAY LIFE

When you, after a long and tiring day, put on your slippers and watch Celebrity Big Brother on TV, you are probably acting wrongly.

There will almost always be opportunities to produce greater good: meet a lonely relative, talk to your depressed neighbour, do some charity work etc. (I ignore the possibility that the TV show is so bad that it is bad for you to watch it.) Is it sensible to say that you violate your moral duty whenever you spend a quiet evening at home in front of the TV? This would be a heavy duty indeed. We are all wrongdoers when we are relaxing.

In these cases, we seem to think that to maximize goodness is beyond the call of duty. It is a morally desirable thing to do but it is not something you ought to do. Another way to sum up the problem is to say that utilitarianism does not give people *options*; it does not allow the agent to pursue his interests at the expense of the overall good.

In this chapter I will first go through some of the standard utilitarian responses to these cases. I will then consider how demanding utilitarianism is in comparison to other non-utilitarian moral theories. In the final section, I will discuss the objection that utilitarianism is so demanding that it cannot be reconciled with true friendship.

UTILITARIAN RESPONSES

(a) Ought entails can

The utilitarian could try to lessen the blow by pointing out that only heroes can perform heroic acts. Normal people do not have the guts and strength to perform heroic actions. For instance, paralyzed by fear, you might not be able to go back into the burning building to save the second child. But if this is so, then you are not obligated to act heroically, for ought entails can.

One obvious reply is to say that even if you are unable, in your present state, to perform heroic actions, you could still change yourself gradually over time and acquire the ability to perform heroic actions. However, this assumes a very optimistic picture of humans. It is doubtful that we can all become moral saints given the right training. Many of us would just make things worse if we tried. The pessimistic utilitarian would therefore say that we ought not even try to become saints.

No matter whether this pessimism is warranted, the 'ought entails can' reply can in any case only provide a partial answer, since there are many cases, the charity case above being one example, where it is clearly possible for us to sacrifice a lot in our lives for the sake of the overall good.

(b) Distinguish wrongness from blameworthiness

A more general response that seems to take most of the sting out of the objection is to deny that wrongness entails blameworthiness. The utilitarian claim that we are almost always doing wrong is especially hard to accept if one assumes that all wrongdoers are blameworthy. Now, it is easy to deny that wrongness entails blameworthiness if blameworthiness is understood as 'ought to be blamed' and blaming is, in turn, understood as an act of 'telling someone off'. It is clear that utilitarianism does not say that we should always tell wrong-doers off, for telling a wrongdoer off is an action that will often only make things worse.

But this understanding of blameworthiness is questionable. To judge that someone is blameworthy seems more like an assessment of *him* than an assessment of an *act* directed towards him. Indeed, it seems possible for someone to be blameworthy even though no one can 'tell him off'. Hitler is still blameworthy, but since he is dead we can no longer tell him off. Similarly, an evil person who has fallen into a coma can still be blameworthy even if no one can tell him off (and get the message across).

This complication need not worry the utilitarian, however, because he simply can take it on board: To say that an act is wrong is to assess the act, not the agent. So, when the utilitarian is saying that you do wrong when you relax in front of the TV, he is not saying that you are blameworthy, for to say that an agent is blameworthy is to assess the agent, not the act.

But this reaction is in fact too hasty. Even if wrongness and blame-worthiness are different concepts that apply to different things, there can still be necessary connections between these concepts. In particu-lar, we have not yet ruled out that if I do something wrong, I must be blameworthy. We need a positive argument against such a connection.

One such argument has to do with moral excuses. Sometimes we have a good excuse for why we acted wrongly. But if we have a good excuse, we are not blameworthy. Suppose that, walking down the street one day, you see a person apparently stabbing another with a knife, and you try to stop this by hitting the attacker. Now, the apparent assault was in fact only play-acting in a street theatre performance, but you could not have known this at the time. Your injuring the actor seems wrong, but since you had no clue that it was only a staged attack, you are not blameworthy.[1]

Of course, there are still cases where we do seem to know that we are not maximizing the good and thus know that we are doing wrong according to utilitarianism. For example, when you are relaxing in front of the TV you may in fact know that you could do more good by calling a friend in distress or help your neighbour with babysitting. So, the utilitarian is pressed to offer a more general response.

One such response would be to say that even if we concede that knowingly doing wrong merits blame, how much blame it merits depends in part on how costly the action would be to the agent. If helping your friend would only require a quick phone call, then not calling your friend merits more blame than it would in a situation where helping your friend would require spending a whole day and night with him. Similarly, if you let your friends die when you could have saved them by sacrificing your life, you have done wrong, but since the costs to you of doing right would have been enormous, you do not merit much blame. Indeed, one might even think that you do not merit any blame for your wrongdoing, since you have a very good excuse.

(c) Morality is demanding but not overriding

The utilitarian could ask us whether we really know the reasons for our worry that utilitarianism is too demanding. Are we sure it is a *moral* worry? Do we question utilitarianism because of its demanding moral requirements, or because these moral requirements are supposed to override all other non-moral requirements, including requirements of prudence, friendship, and parenthood? Perhaps the crux of the matter is that we implicitly assume that utilitarianism tells us that *all things considered* we ought to sacrifice a lot in our lives. But this follows only if we accept:

Overridingness
In deciding what to do *all things considered,* moral reasons overrides any other kind of reason.

If this thesis is denied, the utilitarians could say that it is true that morality is very demanding but there are non-moral reasons that sometimes override moral reasons. For instance, even if morality requires you to sacrifice your life in order to save your friends, prudence might override morality in this case so that you are not required, all things considered, to sacrifice your life. A utilitarian who denies the overridingness thesis can therefore claim that your all things considered requirement will not be too demanding.

However, the overridingness thesis seems compelling, for what is the all-things-considered ought if not the moral ought?

(d) Reject maximizing, accept satisficing

One reason why utilitarianism is so demanding is that it tells us to maximize value, to do the best you can. The right remedy might thus be to lower the standards and say that you are only obligated to do what is *sufficiently* good, not what is best:

> *Satisficing utilitarianism*
> An action ought to be done if and only if it would bring about a sufficient level of total well-being.[2]

To make this theory more precise, we need to decide on a non-maximal level of total well-being, w, that counts as sufficient in the circumstances. This theory might look promising, since it allows you to choose between the actions that will produce a sufficient amount of good (at least as much as w), and thus permits you to pursue your interests at the expense of some overall good.

But satisficing utilitarianism will in fact not solve the problem with heavy duty, for the agent is still required to produce an outcome with the overall well-being of at least w, no matter how much this will cost the agent. So, for instance, if the agent can produce an outcome with w amount of total well-being only if he makes a big sacrifice, he is required to do so. The root of the problem is that w is still defined as a sum of total well-being. So, in order to avoid this problem, we have to somehow single out the *agent's* sacrifice and give it extra weight when we define the sufficient level of total well-being. But this runs counter to impartiality – the agent's well-being should be given the same weight as the well-being of any other person – and so is not an option for utilitarians.

(e) Utilitarianism is not as demanding as we might think

Contrary to appearance, utilitarianism does not imply that you should walk through life like a pained do-gooder constantly trying to save people from illnesses and death. There are three reasons for this.

First, you will be burnt out if you are constantly trying to promote well-being. Charity workers often complain about how hard it is to be surrounded by ill and dying people. Even Mother Theresa, who is often seen as a moral saint, admitted in her diaries that she often suffered from depression. Now, giving yourself some periods of relaxation will not just do you some good but will also do other people good, since it will make you a more efficient promoter of total well-being. We tend to miss this obvious fact because we think about our options as immediate one-shot actions: Should I *now* save this child from illness? Should I *now* donate one pound to charity? But our options often include plans of actions that stretch into the future. So, the question is not whether I should now donate this pound or save this child; the question is whether I should include in my plan for the future a certain amount of charity work. If I do not leave any time for relaxation in my plan, I will be exhausted and do less good overall. The best plan available to me will contain an optimal balance of periods of relaxation – 'me' time – and periods of charity work. How this balance will look may differ from one person to another depending on skills, motivation, and knowledge.

Second, freelance do-gooders need not be the best promoters of well-being. It is often more efficient to unite and act together to change crucial political and economic structures that prevent poor and ill people from flourishing. For example, instead of sending almost all of your salary to Oxfam every month you should get together with others and put pressure on your government to write off poor countries' international debts.

Third, you may be able to change your character and values so that helping others in need becomes one of your deepest projects. Of course, this is not a change that will happen over night. You can only do it indirectly by implementing a long-term plan, which may involve finding out more about poor people's needs and joining a local charity organization. Now, the more you desire to do good, the less burdensome it will be. You will of course be forced to sacrifice a lot of time, energy, and comfort, but you do not have to sacrifice all of your deepest projects since doing good will now be one of them.

Also, the more you desire to do good things, the more likely it is that you will succeed in doing good, since success depends partly on motivation. Utilitarianism will therefore tell you to work against world poverty *and form an interest in doing it.*

NON-UTILITARIAN DEMANDS

You may not be convinced by these responses. But it is important to keep in mind that non-utilitarian moralities are quite demanding too. For instance, it is not clear that they will avoid the 'chocolate versus charity' problem. It is not just utilitarians who think we should rather save a child from illness than buy a piece of chocolate. Surely, any plausible non-utilitarian theory must accept that it is, other things being equal, better to save a life than to enjoy a piece of chocolate. But then, if this reasoning is repeated, we get the result that the agent becomes poor, since small sacrifices will eventually add up to a big sacrifice.

Some non-utilitarian moralities threaten to be as demanding as utilitarianism. For example, a virtue ethics that tells you to do what the fully virtuous person would do is potentially very demanding. It all depends on how the fully virtuous person is defined. If he is in the league of Gandhi, Jesus, and Mother Theresa, we will have a very demanding theory that tells you to endure great sacrifices for the sake of others.

Of course, the virtue ethicist could respond by saying that the fully virtuous person should be seen as an *ideal* for us to emulate in our actions as much as possible. The closer our actions resemble this ideal, the better they are. But the utilitarian can say something similar. The fully impartial and benevolent agent can also be seen as an ideal. The closer your actions resemble this ideal, that is, the more total well-being you produce, the better your actions are. Now, there is a general worry here that the notions 'right' and 'wrong' would no longer have any role to play. However, if this is a real worry, then it is as much a worry for virtue ethics as it is for utilitarianism. Notice, for instance, that if the virtue ethicist responds to this worry by equating the right action with the ideal, then all actions falling short of the ideal will be wrong, and he would have to agree with the utilitarians that most of us are wrongdoers most of the time. Of course, he could still say that there are degrees of wrongdoing – ethnic cleansing is a more serious wrong than a white lie. It is thus a mistake to think that nothing matters just because we are all wrongdoers most of the time. There are better and worse sinners. But, again, this option is open to the utilitarian as well.

Kantianism cannot avoid the demandingness problem either, since it imposes a strong prohibition against deception; you are not allowed to lie even if this is the only way to protect your vital interests. Indeed, according to Kant, you are not allowed to lie even if this is the only way to save your friends or loved ones from being killed by the enemy soldier who is asking you where they are hiding.

BEYOND THE CALL OF DUTY

Still, there seems to be one important difference between utilitarian demands and non-utilitarian demands. Utilitarians cannot accept that there are *supererogatory* actions, actions that are morally desirable, but go beyond the call of duty. Non-utilitarians, in contrast, can accept such actions, since they can reject the consequentialist idea that you ought to do the best you can.

It is true that we do often describe actions as going beyond the call of duty, but it is in fact not clear how to make sense of this talk. The supererogatory action is supposed to be better in some sense than the action you ought to perform. But if 'better' means 'more moral reason to do', we have a problem. We would have to say that you are morally permitted to do something even though you have more moral reason to do something else. This sounds paradoxical.

One way to avoid this paradoxical situation is to make use of the distinction between wrongness and blameworthiness we discussed earlier. You *should* or *ought* do the supererogatory action, but you do not *have* to. You ought to do it, because this is what you have most moral reason to do. But you do not have to do it in order to avoid blame. So, although failing to save the second child in the burning building is wrong, it does not make you blameworthy, for you have a very good excuse (third-degree burns). You ought to save her but you do not have to.

This way of avoiding the paradox would of course be welcomed by utilitarians and consequentialists, since they are keen to distinguish wrongness from blameworthiness. If it can be made to work, utilitarians will be able to accommodate supererogatory actions after all.

CAN UTILITARIANS BE GOOD FRIENDS?

Some people think that the answer is clearly no. It is not just that utilitarians do not make good friends; they do not make friends at all. This would be a serious objection to utilitarianism, since loving relationships and friendships are among the most important factors in a good life, a life worth living. So, if utilitarianism requires agents to lead lives that are not worth living, it is surely an all too demanding theory. But is it really true that utilitarians cannot be friends? To answer this question, let us set up a dialogue between a utilitarian and a critic, who used to think they were friends.

The critic: I hope you agree that if you are my genuine friend, you value and love me as an *end*. You value me for what I am over and above the usefulness of being your friend. And you do things for my sake, not just for the sake of some other value. If you value me merely as a useful acquaintance, who can help you out in different ways, then you are not a genuine friend. How can you then be my friend? As a genuine utilitarian, you have only one fundamental aim in your life: to make the world a better place. So there cannot be any room for other commitments in your life. In particular, there can be no room for friendship.

The utilitarian: I agree with your analysis of friendship. But it is a misunderstanding to think that my utilitarian theory prevents me from pursuing other ends and interests. My utilitarian theory does allow me to be your true friend. You fail to distinguish between utilitarianism seen as a *decision method* and utilitarianism seen as a *criterion of rightness*. Utilitarianism is first of all a criterion of rightness. It tells you what makes an action right or wrong. This is not the same thing as a method of deliberation which tells you what you should aim at and how you should deliberate when you decide what to do. Since I believe in utilitarianism, I believe that what makes an action right is that it has optimal consequences in terms of overall well-being. But I do not believe that I should constantly be preoccupied with utilitarian calculations. For this will itself have consequences, and sometimes bad consequences. This applies to friendship as well. I think that the world is a better world when people have relationships like ours and, as you have pointed out, I could not have this relationship if I constantly made utilitarian calculations. I would make things worse if I took an instrumental attitude towards my friendships and always applied the utilitarian test to them. Of course, this is not to give up utilitarianism. For I still have a standing commitment to lead the life that will have the best consequences overall. I would seek to lead a different sort of life if I did not think that this life promoted overall well-being.

The critic: But how can you value me as an end when you would happily end our friendship if you thought it would not be conducive to overall well-being. Your commitment to utilitarianism will always *override* your commitment to me. This shows that you are not my friend.

The utilitarian: No, you confuse the notion of commitment to an end *for its own sake* with that of an *overriding* commitment. I do value you as an end even though I do not value you as an overriding end. Not all ends are overriding. For instance, I am sure that in a choice between ending our relationship and causing horrible suffering to your kids, you would choose to end our relationship. But this does not show that you are not my friend. Does it?

The critic: OK, you may be right about this. But there is still a contingency involved in your attitude towards me that prevents you from valuing our friendship as an end. Look, you are telling me that

(a) you value me as an end.

But since you are a utilitarian it is also true that

(b) you value me only so long as valuing me promotes overall well-being.

But to value me for my own sake is to value me for what I am in myself, in virtue of who I am. So, (a) is incompatible with (b).

The utilitarian: Your analysis of what it is to value someone for their own sake is correct, but you apply it incorrectly. (b) does not say that I take an instrumental attitude towards you. It says that my attitude is *contingent* on its promoting overall good. It says that my intrinsic attitude towards you meets a certain *counterfactual* condition: I would not hold this attitude if it did not promote the overall good. And there is nothing strange in saying that an intrinsic attitude is contingent in this way. Consider a tennis player who desperately wants to win. It is self-defeating for him to think, 'No matter how

I play, the only thing I care about is whether I win.' He should instead devote himself more to the game and the play as such. Assume that he spends a good deal of time developing a devotion to the play as such so the following is now true of him.

(c) He values playing the game for its own sake.

Then it is not true that he values the game instrumentally. But this does not mean that his initial goal to win is inconsistent with his devotion to the play. For his desire to win can still be *an ultimate organizing desire* for his other desires. If this desire is effective, the following will be true about him.

(d) He values playing the game only so long as valuing the game promotes his winning.

His intrinsic devotion to the play is *contingent* on his winning the games. If this motivational structure is possible in the case of tennis playing, it must be possible in the case of friendship.[3]

The critic: Well, I am not a tennis game, am I? I am a person. I am not fully convinced. Perhaps you can value me as an end. So perhaps you can even be my friend after all. But you are not an especially good friend I must say. You say that you value me for my own sake. But you do not value me *wholeheartedly*. To value someone whole-heartedly is not just to value that person for her own sake but also to intrinsically endorse that very attitude. It is to have an intrinsic posi-tive attitude towards your first attitude. Your first-order attitude requires a second-order intrinsic endorsement. In other words,

(e) If you *wholeheartedly* value me as an end, then you intrinsically endorse the fact that you value me as an end.

Compare with a drug addict who loves the high for its own sake but intrinsically hates the fact that he loves the high. He does not want to be a person who loves the high. This person does not wholeheartedly love his high, for he does not intrinsically endorse his love for the drug. Or take the case with the kleptomaniac who loves the rush he experiences when he shoplifts, but hates the fact that he loves this rush. He does not wholeheartedly value this rush because he does not intrinsically endorse the fact that he likes the rush. It is the same with you and your attitudes towards me. For you only value your first-order attitude towards me *instrumentally*, only so long as it promotes goodness. So, you cannot value me wholeheartedly. You do not endorse the fact that you value me as an end.

The utilitarian: No this is not right. First of all, your definition of what it is to wholeheartedly value something is too demanding. Look at the case with the drug addict. He hates the fact that he loves the high. But my attitudes towards you are different. I do not hate the fact that I value you as an end. So, the right characterization of a wholehearted engagement is

(f) If I *wholeheartedly* value you as an end, then I do not intrinsically hate the fact that I value you as an end.

Furthermore, my consequentialist commitment does not prevent me from intrinsically endorsing the fact that I value you as an end. For this second-order attitude might be the attitude that promotes the overall good in the long run. I am inclined to think so. The world would be a worse place if I did not intrinsically endorse the fact that I love you as an end. My commitment to you would not be strong enough to promote the good things that come out of an intimate friendship.

You have been questioning me. Let me now ask you something. If you are right in your accusations then all moral agents seem to have a problem no matter which moral theory they believe in. For your criticism can of course be generalized. You seem to think that it is impossible to combine the following two claims:

I value you for your own sake
I value you only so long as this promotes the overall goodness.

But your argument works even if we replace the utilitarian moral goal with a non-utilitarian one:

I value you for your own sake.
I value you only so long as this satisfies the non-utilitarian moral principle P.

For P we can put any non-utilitarian moral principle. For instance, P can be Kant's categorical imperative, or some set of deontological principles, the Ten Commandments, a virtue theory, or what have you. So if you are right, then moral theory in general is in trouble. You cannot be deeply committed to a moral theory if you want to be a good friend. But that seems to be a reductio of your argument.

The critic: No, this is not true. Now *you* are conflating things. It is true that some moral theories will give moral agents a hard time being friends. But not all. It depends on the contents of these theories. I, for one, think that an acceptable moral principle must explicitly and directly allow me to value people as ends and act on these values. For instance, I should be permitted to spend time with my friends instead of making sure that a bunch of strangers spend time with their friends. Also, I should be permitted to visit my friend at the hospital even though I know that the lonely guy next door would benefit more from a visit. What is wrong with utilitarianism is that it cannot allow these actions. Your theory is too impartial.

The utilitarian: But a moral principle should be impartial. We should give equal considerations to all people. This is what it means to be moral. So I am not convinced. But I think you have at least convinced me that one should not discuss the value of friendship if one wants to keep one's friends. It may be impossible to be friends with a utilitarian who tries to convince you that she can be a good friend.

CONCLUDING REMARKS

There is no way around it, utilitarianism is a demanding moral theory. Utilitarianism implies that we are all moral underachievers, since we often fail to maximize total well-being. However, even if it is true that we often act wrongly, it is not clear that this also means that we are blameworthy, for in many cases, we do have a good excuse for doing wrong (we did not know it was wrong, or the right action would have been very costly to us). But it is doubtful that we have a good excuse for not giving more to charity and for not spending more time and energy on helping the needy. So, utilitarianism will definitely blame us for not being more other-regarding in our actions. Of course, no one doubts that being more other-regarding is praiseworthy and morally desirable, but the question is whether this is what we ought to do.

However, utilitarianism is not alone in being a demanding moral theory. Both virtue ethics and Kantianism can make tough demands on agents. Even common-sense morality, which is usually supposed to be pretty easy on moral agents, does ask for great sacrifices if reasonable demands are repeated over time. So, it seems that any plausible moral theory will be demanding. I leave it to you to decide whether utilitarianism is too demanding.

SUGGESTED READING

On the demandingness objection:

Cullity, G. (2004), *The Moral Demands of Affluence*, Oxford: Clarendon Press.

Mulgan, T. (2001), *The Demands of Consequentialism*, Oxford: Oxford University Press.

Singer, P. (1972), 'Famine, affluence, and morality', *Philosophy and Public Affairs*, Vol. 1, No. 3, 229–243.

On blameless wrongdoing:

Parfit, D. (1993), *Reasons and Persons*, Oxford: Oxford University Press, Part 1, Chapter 1, Section 14.

Tännsjö, T. (1998), *Hedonistic Utilitarianism*, Edinburgh: Edinburgh University Press, Chapter 9.

On the notion of going beyond the call of duty (supererogation):

Heyd, D. (1982), *Supererogation: Its Status in Ethical Theory*, Cambridge: Cambridge University Press.

Zimmerman, M. (1994), *The Concept of Moral Obligation*, New York: Cambridge University Press, Chapter 8.

On friendship and utilitarianism:

Railton, P. (1984), 'Alienation, consequentialism, and the demands of morality', *Philosophy and Public Affairs*, Vol. 13, No. 2, 134–171.

Scanlon, T. M. (1998), *What We Owe to Each Other*, Cambridge, MA: Harvard University Press, 88–89.

CHAPTER EIGHT

IS UTILITARIANISM TOO PERMISSIVE?

We have seen that utilitarianism can be accused of being too demanding since it does not give us any *options*; it does not allow us to pursue our innocent projects at the expense of overall well-being. But utilitarianism can also be accused of being too permissive, because it rejects both *constraints* on actions and *special duties* to our nearest and dearest. It rejects constraints on actions, since any action, no matter how morally repugnant, can be obligatory. We just need to imagine a case in which a repugnant action happens to maximize total well-being. For instance, I am allowed to torture an innocent person if this is the only way for me to promote overall well-being. Utilitarianism rejects special duties as well, since impartial benevolence cannot admit of any exceptions in favour of some people over others. So, for example, I am permitted to save the stranger's child rather than my own, if the stranger's child would benefit more.

In this chapter I shall consider the utilitarian responses to these objections. In particular, I shall give an explanation of why classical utilitarianism is unable to accommodate constraints and special duties. This will enable us to see whether other forms of utilitarianism can do a better job at accounting for constraints and special duties.

CONSTRAINTS

Examples of constraints embraced by common-sense morality as well as many deontological theories are,

Do not lie!
Keep your promises!

Do not kill innocent persons!
Do not torture!
Do not punish the innocent!

All deontologists agree that constraints cannot easily be overridden by considerations about well-being. You are forbidden to violate them even if this is the only way to promote total well-being. Are you *never* allowed to violate them? Here deontologists differ in their views. Some think these constraints are absolute so that you are never, under any possible circumstances, allowed to violate a constraint. Others think a constraint can be violated when it comes into conflict with a more important constraint. Perhaps you are allowed to lie in order to avoid breaking an important promise. Still others go even further and think that a constraint can be violated when enough total well-being is at stake. Perhaps you are allowed to kill one innocent person in order to prevent a nuclear holocaust.

Since utilitarianism does not accept any constraints on actions (except, trivially, the constraint to maximize total well-being), it can be accused of being too permissive. Here are some vivid examples, listed in order of increasing repugnancy.

The promise

You have promised to return a book to your friend. But you realize that your lonely neighbour would benefit a lot from reading it. So, you decide to give the book to your neighbour instead of returning it to your friend. Utilitarianism would approve of your action if you benefited your neighbour more than you harmed your friend.[1]

The car accident

One winter, you have had a car accident on a lonely road. The other passenger is badly injured. You find an isolated house occupied by an old woman and her grandchild. There is no phone, but a car in the garage. You ask to borrow it. She does not trust you and is so terrified that she locks herself inside the bathroom leaving the child outside the bathroom. The only way to persuade her to lend you her car is to twist the child's arm so that she can hear the child scream. Utilitarianism says that you ought to twist the child's arm, since it would be worse to let the injured passenger die.[2]

The judge

A murder has been committed and most people believe that Jake is guilty, but the judge knows he is innocent. If the judge does not get Jake hanged, there will be a riot and several people will die. Utilitarianism says that the judge ought to sentence the innocent Jake to death since causing one to be killed is better than allowing many to be killed.[3]

The transplant

A doctor has five patients who will all die if they do not get an immediate transplant. One patient needs a new heart, two need a new lung, and two need a new kidney. By sheer coincidence, the doctor finds out that a healthy person, who is in hospital for a routine check-up, happens to be the perfect donor for all five patients. Utilitarianism would tell the doctor to cut up the healthy person and distribute the organs to the five patients, since that would maximize total well-being.[4]

UTILITARIAN RESPONSES

A common utilitarian reply is to concede that there are no constraints, but claim that, normally, it is wrong to lie, break promises, kill, and harm the innocent, for these actions will not normally maximize total well-being. It is only in special circumstances that total-well-being is maximized by violating these principles. So, the utilitarian will honour these principles as important rules of thumb rather than constraints on actions. If you follow these principles, you will normally maximize total well-being.

There may even be a good utilitarian argument for adopting a policy of not even thinking about the most repugnant violations as viable options. For instance, it might be better if a judge adopts a policy of not even entertaining the option of punishing the innocent, since such thinking may very well lead to bad consequences. A judge who sees punishing the innocent as 'just another option' will be less sensitive to the rules of law and, since it is difficult for the judge to fake it, this will tend to erode people's trust in law and order. Furthermore, a judge can easily misjudge the situation. Is it certain that the riot can be prevented only by sentencing an innocent person to death? Can he not, for instance, somehow pretend to have him executed instead? And what about the reactions of the friends and family of the innocent person who is killed?

Similarly, a doctor who is always on the look out for healthy patients to cut up and use as (unwilling) donors has adopted a policy that tends to have very grave consequences in the long run. If people get to know about his policy, they will lose all trust in the doctor and avoid visits to the hospital even when they have an urgent need to be treated. Furthermore, the doctor can easily misjudge the situation. Is it, for instance, so clear that no one will know about his enforced donations? And is it clear that killing one will in fact lead to a full recovery of all his other patients? Aren't there other better policies to consider, for instance, encouraging people to donate their organs after their death so that there will be no need to kill one patient in order to save others?

For less abhorrent violations, such as lying and breaking promises, the utilitarian could claim that it may be better to adopt a policy of thinking of them as actions one 'must not do', at least in situations where no catastrophic outcomes are at stake. This can be compared to the way dieters should think about whether to have another piece of cake. Of course, one more piece of cake will not in itself do any harm, but if you take this to heart and always give yourself the permission to have another piece of cake, it is more likely that you will end up eating the whole cake. It may be better to think 'I must not have another piece of cake' even though you know that another piece of cake would not in fact cause you any harm. Analogously, even if a particular lie would not harm anyone, if you start giving yourself permission to lie whenever you cannot see any harm coming, you will weaken your general commitment to honesty and that will have bad consequences in the long run. Indeed, one might even argue that in order to succesfully participate in the promise institution in the first place you have to block out thinking in terms of small benefits and losses of keeping a promise. If you are constantly calculating the pros and cons of keeping your promise to me, you will no longer be playing the promise game.

One could complain that this utilitarian policy will split the mind of the moral agent, since he will think in ways he knows are false. Indeed, one might worry that it will lead to flat-out inconsistency in his beliefs: he believes that there are no constraints *and* that breaking a promise is simply forbidden. But perhaps the agent does not have to believe that promise breaking is wrong in order to reap the good consequences of his promise-keeping strategy. The smoker who is trying to kick his habit can combat his urge to smoke by thinking that smoking will certainly kill him when in fact he knows that this is an exaggeration and that there is only a non-negligible probability that he will die from smoking. Perhaps the utilitarian agent can do something similar in his pursuit of total well-being. His strategy is to exaggerate and think 'This is simply impermissible' in cases where he can easily break a promise.

Of course, these replies do nothing to block the conclusion that utilitarianism will sometimes tell you to do repugnant things, for, strictly speaking, there are no constraints and special duties. These replies will only show that the best utilitarian policy is often not to consider the repugnant actions at all or, when you do consider them, to think about them as actions you must not do.

SPECIAL OBLIGATIONS TO OUR NEAREST AND DEAREST

Common-sense morality and many deontologist theories embrace special duties to our near and dear, including duties to our friends, family members (parents, siblings, children . . .), partners (wives, husbands . . .), and fellow members of your community. These duties are grounded in facts about our relations to others. They differ from constraints in that special duties are owed to some people but not to others, depending on which relationship we stand to them. For instance, I owe it to my children to shelter them simply because they are my children. Constraints, however, are owed to anyone (if they are owed at all). I should not torture an innocent person, no matter whether he is a friend, child, parent, or a stranger.

Since special duties are supposed to sometimes override considerations about well-being, the utilitarian cannot accept these duties. For instance, in the choice between saving your child and some stranger's child, you are required to save the stranger's child, if that would produce more total well-being. No special weight is given to the fact that one of the children is your child.

UTILITARIAN RESPONSES

As in the case of constraints, the utilitarian can argue that special duties are good rules of thumb. There are several reasons why it is often a good utilitarian policy to show more concern for your nearest and dearest. Sidgwick pointed out the following three reasons.[5] First, we tend to derive more pleasures from interactions with our nearest and dearest than from interactions with complete strangers. Taking out a friend for dinner is more enjoyable than taking out a stranger. Second, we often have more knowledge about how to benefit our nearest and dearest than how to benefit strangers, since we know more about our friends' tastes and preferences than those of strangers. Third, we are often in a better situation to distribute benefits to our nearest and dearest. I can more easily visit my ill friend than visit an ill stranger far away.

So, the utilitarian can argue that special duties and utilitarian duties often coincide. However, the coincidence is far from perfect, especially in our modern society where we have both the information and the technological means necessary to help perfect strangers far away. Since many of these strangers are in great distress – they are starving, ill, or very poor – the choice between taking your friend out for dinner and sending the equivalent sum of money to a trustworthy charity should be clear to the utilitarian. Here the demandingness objection to utilitarianism reappears.

There is, however, another way for the utilitarian to make room for special duties. Instead of seeing them as moral duties, he could see them as *non-moral* requirements stemming from certain perfectionist values. In general, something has perfectionist value if it is a good instance of its kind. So, for example, a knife that cuts well is a good instance of its kind and, therefore, a good knife ought to cut well. By the same reasoning, one could say:

a good friend ought to give priority to his friends,
a good parent ought to give priority to his children,
a good partner ought to give priority to his partner, and
a good community member ought to give priority to his community.

Now, if these requirements are normative in the sense that they provide non-moral reason to act, and if these reasons are strong enough to sometimes trump moral ones, utilitarians can happily accept that we sometimes have more overall reason to be a good parent than to do what is morally right, and, therefore, more reason to save our own child rather than a stranger's child.

But this response is convincing only if it is reasonable to reject the thesis that moral reasons are overriding, and, as we noted in the previous chapter, this is controversial. Furthermore, this response still denies that we have *moral* reasons to be partial towards our nearest and dearest, and this is counter-intuitive.

CAN CONSTRAINTS AND SPECIAL OBLIGATIONS BE BUILT INTO THE GOOD?

We have seen that utilitarianism is forced to reject constraints and special duties. At most, it can accept that constraints and special duties have instrumental value. This, no doubt, makes utilitarianism a less intuitive moral theory. But recall that what we have in mind here is *classical* utilitarianism. It is therefore important to ask whether there is another version of utilitarianism that could accommodate constraints and special duties. I shall argue that the answer is both yes and no.

To see why an affirmative answer seems right, consider again the example about the car accident now put in a diagrammatical form in Table 8.1. (For simplicity, I ignore the well-being of you and the woman. We can assume that you and the woman would suffer to the same degree no matter what you did.)

Classical utilitarianism says that the child ought to be tortured since this will maximize the total sum of well-being (-5 compared to -10). But other versions of utilitarianism need not have this implication. For instance, the fact that a person is intentionally harmed can be assigned negative intrinsic value. It is not just bad for a person to suffer; it is also bad for a person that he is intentionally and knowingly harmed. If this more objective conception of well-being is

Table 8.1

Actions	Outcome 1	Total value
Twist the child's arm	The child suffers (-5) Your passenger is saved (0)	$-5 + 0 = -5$
Not twist the child's arm	The child does not suffer (0) Your passenger is left to suffer (-10)	$0 - 10 = -10$

Table 8.2

Actions	Outcome 1	Outcome 2	Total value
Twist the child's arm	The child suffers (−5) Your passenger is saved (0)	The child is intentionally harmed (−10)	−5 + 0 − 10 = −15
Not twist the child's arm	The child does not suffer (0) Your passenger is left to suffer (−10)	The child is not intentionally harmed (0)	0 −10 + 0 = −10

accepted, utilitarianism can say that we ought to refrain from torturing the child, as Table 8.2 shows.

In this example, not twisting the child's arm will maximize value (−10 compared to −15.) Similar reasoning applies to the other deontological constraints: telling a lie, breaking a promise, and punishing the innocent can all be assigned intrinsic disvalue. Of course, it will sometimes be difficult to provide a plausible story that explains why being violated in some of these ways, being lied to, for instance, must *in itself* be bad for oneself. The non-utilitarian consequentialist, however, need not be worried by this, since he can accept that something is bad without it being bad for anyone. So, even if utilitarians will be hard-pressed to come up with a good justification for all constraints, the non-utilitarian consequentialist may have an easier time providing such a justification.[6]

To see how a non-classical utilitarian can incorporate special obligations to our nearest and dearest, consider again the case of the drowning children. Your child has been playing in the water with a stranger's child and they have now drifted out into deep waters. They are both drowning but, unfortunately, you can only save one. See Table 8.3.

Table 8.3

Options	Outcome
Save your child, let the other child drown	Your child is saved and leads a happy life
Save the other child, let your own child drown	The other child is saved and leads a happy life

Table 8.4

Options	Outcome 1	Outcome 2	Total value
Save your child, let the other child drown	Your child is saved and leads a happy life (10)	Your child is saved by his parent (5)	10 + 5 = 15
Save the other child, let your own child drown	The other child is saved and leads a happy life (10)	The other child is not saved by his parent (0)	10 + 0 = 10

Classical utilitarianism says that both actions are right, if the children's happiness would be the same and the parents' suffering would be the same. But other versions of utilitarianism need not say this. The fact that a child is saved by her own parent can be assigned positive intrinsic value. More generally, it is good that children are saved by their parents because this expresses the intrinsic value of parental care. This is consistent with utilitarianism if we add that it is *good in itself for children* to be the object of parental care. If this more objective conception of well-being is accepted, then even utilitarianism can say that you ought to save your child, as Table 8.4 shows.

Similar reasoning applies to the other special obligations. Again, non-utilitarian consequentialist may have an easier time providing a plausible justification for taking into account the values of special duties, since they do not have to say that these values are necessarily part of someone's well-being.

So far so good, but here is still a sense in which utilitarianism, indeed any form of consequentialism, is unable to incorporate both constraints and special obligations. Defenders of constraints often claim that you are not allowed to violate a constraint in order to prevent other violations of the same constraint. This means, for instance, that you are not allowed to torture one person in order to prevent others from torturing, and you are not allowed to break one promise in order to prevent others from breaking promises. Similarly, defenders of special obligations claim that you are not allowed to violate a special duty in order to prevent other violations of the same special duty. So, you are not allowed to violate your duty to your child in order to prevent others from violating their duties to their children.

This feature of constraints and special duties prevent the utilitarian and, more generally, any kind of consequentialist, from accommodating them. To see this in the case of constraints, consider the schematic example in Table 8.5.

Assume that if I torture A, you will spare B. But if I do not torture A, you will torture B. Now, a torture-sensitive consequentialism could assign intrinsic disvalue to the fact that someone is tortured (and a utilitarian could add that it is in itself bad for someone to be tortured). But this theory will not forbid me to torture A, if the involved torturings are equally bad. For then the outcomes will contain the same good and bad things: that one person is not tortured and that another person is tortured. The outcomes of my options must therefore have the same value and I am thus permitted to torture A. For a consequentialist, it cannot matter that someone is tortured by *me*. What matters is that *someone* is tortured by *someone*. Analogous reasons apply to the other constraints.

The similarly structured example in Table 8.6 shows that no consequentialist can accommodate special duties. Assume that if I save my child, this will prevent you from saving your child, and if I do not save my child, you will save yours. A parental duty-sensitive consequentialist that assigns intrinsic value to the fact that a parent saves his child (and perhaps adds that this is good for the child) will not require me to save my child, since the outcomes of my options

Table 8.5

My options	Outcomes
I torture A	A is tortured, you do not torture B
I do not torture A	A is not tortured, you torture B

Table 8.6

My options	Outcomes
I save my child	My child is saved by me, you do not save your child
I do not save my child	My child is not saved, you save your child

are equal in value. The outcomes contain the same good and bad things: that one child is saved by his parent and that another child is not saved by his parent. For a consequentialist, it cannot matter that *I* save *my* child. What matters is that a child is saved by her parent. Analogous reasons apply to the other special duties.

We now have a clear explanation for why utilitarianism and, more generally, consequentialism, cannot accommodate constraints and special duties. According to all forms of consequentialism, the agent's relation to a violation of a constraint or a special duty does not matter. It does not matter whether *he* is violating the constraint or the special duty. It only matters that these violations would be brought about by his actions. By contrast, according to common sense and many deontologists, the fact that you will violate a constraint or a special duty provides a special reason for you not to violate the constraint or the special duty. This is sometimes summed up in the slogan that consequentialism has no room for *agent-relative* reasons. A constraint-sensitive or special duty-sensitive consequentialism is still agent-neutral in the sense that it does not matter who is doing the killing, the torturing, the promise breaking, or the violation of the special duty. You should simply minimize the number of violations of constraints and special duties, even if that requires that you commit a violation, because violations are intrinsically bad and you should minimize what is bad. The fact that *you* will commit a violation is not morally relevant.

TRADE-OFF PROBLEMS

A constraint-based morality does not allow us to violate constraints whenever that will maximize overall value. But how strict is this constraint supposed to be? Imagine that a lot of suffering is at stake and that the only way to prevent it is to violate a deontological constraint. For example, assume that the only way to avoid the painful end of humanity in a nuclear holocaust is to torture one child. Is it reasonable to say that the constraint against torturing the innocent is sacred even in this extreme situation? This seems too rigid. Even Robert Nozick, a staunch defender of constraints (in fact, he coined the term 'side-constraint'), wavers at this point: 'The question of whether these side-constraints are absolute, or whether they may be violated in order to avoid catastrophic moral horror, and, if the latter, what the resulting structure might look like, is one I hope largely to avoid.'[7] This elusive attitude might be alright given Nozick's purposes in his book *Anarchy, State, and Utopia*. But the question cannot be avoided when constructing a general moral theory.

Of course, we could avoid this rigid view by qualifying the constraints. They should not just read: do not do x. They should contain exception clauses: do not do x, except in circumstances c1, c2 . . . .. But then we need to know how to complete this list. Alternatively, we might say that the constraints are not absolute and allow that given that enough of overall badness is at stake we are allowed to violate the constraint. But then we will have the problem of deciding exactly how much badness must be at stake for us to be allowed to violate the constraints. Where shall we set the threshold?

Deontologists must not just tackle the problem of how to trade constraint violations against the overall good, they also face the problem of how to weigh one constraint violation against another. The deontologist says that we are not allowed to violate one constraint in order to prevent other people from violating constraints. But does he mean that we are not allowed to violate one constraint in order to prevent others from violating *any* kind of constraint? Or does he only mean that we are not allowed to violate one constraint in order to prevent others from violating the *same kind* of constraint?

The first idea is an unreasonably strict theory, for it would not allow me to lie in order to prevent other people from torturing someone, to break a promise in order to prevent someone from killing an innocent person, or to break into someone's house (and thereby damage their property) in order to prevent other people from raping a person. Constraints must therefore be ranked in order of importance, and we should be allowed to violate a less important constraint in order to prevent others from violating constraints that are more important. If this is true, then, of course, the deontologist owes us a justification for treating one constraint as more important than another.

A more important problem is that if this more flexible view is accepted, one can wonder whether even the second idea is acceptable, the idea that I am not allowed to violate a constraint in order to prevent others from violating the *same kind* of constraint. If I am allowed to violate a constraint in order to prevent violations of a slightly less important constraint, why am I not also allowed to violate a constraint in order prevent more violations of the *same* constraint?

CAN CONSTRAINTS AND SPECIAL DUTIES BE JUSTIFIED?

On the face of it, it sounds paradoxical to deny that you can be permitted to commit a violation in order to prevent violations of the same kind. After all, since we think there is something morally undesirable and repugnant about violations, it seems sensible to reduce the number of violations.

The deontologist could reply that this ignores the special role of the agent. It is true that certain acts-types are morally repugnant no matter who performs them, but when a particular agent performs a morally repugnant act, it is *he* who is tainted by the performance of the repugnant act, and thus it is *he* who will bear this moral cost. In contrast, when the agent merely allows other people to do repugnant things, it is they, not he, who will be tainted by doing something repugnant. The agent should therefore avoid the moral cost by refusing to perform a repugnant act even if this means that others will be doing the same kind of repugnant act.

The problem with this reply is that it is too agent-focused: The fundamental reason why an agent should not do something repugnant is that he should not dirty his hands by touching something morally repugnant. As Donald Regan puts it, 'the agent is encouraged to indulge in a sort of Pontius Pilatism, taking the view that as long as he keeps his hands clean, the other agents as well as the consequences can take care of themselves'.[8] But what about the victims who will be allowed to suffer at the hands of other people? Do they have no claim on the agent to be saved from this treatment? To make this objection more vivid, suppose that the only way I can prevent you from being tortured for several days by a group of sadists is by torturing you for a few hours. You are begging me to go ahead and torture you, but I staunchly refuse to do it, since I do not want to be tainted by doing this repugnant act. In this case, I seem to show too much respect for constraints and too little respect for you.

A victim-based deontology would instead say that the reason why I am not allowed to commit a violation in order to prevent other violations is that this is the only way I can respect the true moral status of each person. Each person is *inviolable* in the sense that he cannot be permissibly violated, at least not without his prior consent, in order to prevent similar violations of others. In the example above, I do not impermissibly violate you, because you consented to be tortured by me in order to avoid a greater evil for yourself.

In a case where I can violate you in order to prevent violations of others, it is true that by refraining from violating you I will allow that others are violated. But this does not diminish their moral status, for it is still impermissible to violate them. Moral status defines what we can permissibly do to people, not what actually happens to them. In contrast, if it was permissible for me to violate you in order to prevent violations of others, as utilitarians and consequentialist would have us think, then *everyone's* moral status would be diminished, not just your moral status, for it would now be true that *any* person could be permissibly violated in order to prevent others from being violated. So, on this approach, it is not the fact *I* will do something repugnant and the victim is *mine* that explains why I must not do something repugnant. The explanation is instead that *every* person is inviolable and thus cannot be permissibly violated in order to prevent others from being violated.[9]

This is an intriguing idea, but it should be noted, first, that this kind of inviolability comes in degrees. A person has a maximum degree of inviolability when we are not allowed to violate him no matter how many other violations or how much suffering we could thereby prevent. But such inviolability seems too extreme; it would not allow us to torture one innocent person in order to prevent billions of other people being tortured. Any moderate deontologist who thinks that it is permissible to violate one person when a sufficiently large number of violations or a sufficiently large amount of suffering is at stake would not assign maximum inviolability to people. How much inviolability should we then assign to people? Well, utilitarianism has one answer: no one can be permissibly harmed in order to prevent a lesser amount of harm to others. So, both utilitarians and moderate deontologists assign a less than maximum degree of inviolability to people.

Second, this view simply assumes that moral status is only about what can permissibly be *done* to people. But why isn't moral status also about what can permissibly be *allowed to happen* to people? If you have moral status, how can I be permitted to allow others to violate you? In short, this victim-based approach seems to assume that there is a morally relevant distinction between *doing* and *allowing*. Utilitarians and consequentialists would of course reject such a distinction, since they judge actions by the values of their outcomes, not by the way these outcomes are brought about. In the next chapter, we will take a closer look at the issue whether the way outcomes are brought about makes a moral difference.

CONCLUDING REMARKS

There are no moral 'no go' areas for a utilitarian. Any kind of action, no matter how intuitively repugnant, can be morally right if the choice facing the agent is sufficiently tragic. Also, since everyone counts for one and not for more than one, there is no room for special duties in a utilitarian theory. However, the utilitarian does not deny that *thinking* in terms of constraints and special duties will often have beneficial consequences. So, constraints and special duties can definitively be seen as something instrumentally valuable. They can even be seen as intrinsically valuable if classical utilitarianism is abandoned in favour of a utilitarian theory that adopts a more objective account of well-being (or a non-utilitarian consequentialist theory). But even on this revised utilitarian view, indeed, on any consequentialist view, it is still true that violations of constraints and special duties ought to be minimized, and this may require the agent to 'dirty his hands'. However, it is very difficult to find a plausible explanation of constraints and duties if we maintain that we are never allowed to violate one in order to minimize a great number of similar violations.

SUGGESTED READING

On constraints:

Kamm, F. (2007), *Intricate Ethics*, Oxford: Oxford University Press, 17–23.
Nagel, T. (1986), *The View from Nowhere*, New York: Oxford University Press, 175–180.
Nozick, R. (1974), 'Moral constraints and moral goals', in *Anarchy, State and Utopia*, New York: Basic Books, Chapter 3, 28–30.
Scheffler, S. (1994), *The Rejection of Consequentialism: A Philosophical Investigation of the Considerations Underlying Rival Moral Conceptions*, second revised edition, Oxford: Oxford University Press, esp. Chapters 4–5.

On special obligations:

Jeske, D. (2001), 'Friendship and reasons of intimacy', *Philosophy and Phenomenological Research*, Vol. 63, 329–346.
Scheffler, S. 'Relationships and responsibilities', *Philosophy and Public Affairs*, Vol. 26, 189–209.

On agent-neutral and agent-relative reasons:

Broome, J. (1995), 'Skorupski on agent-neutrality', *Utilitas*, Vol. 7, 315–317.

Nagel, T. (1986), *The View from Nowhere*, New York: Oxford University Press, 152–153, 158–163.
Parfit, D. (1992), *Reasons and Persons*, Oxford: Oxford University Press, 143.

On consequentialism and constraints:

Kagan, S. (1991) 'Replies to My Critics' *Philosophy and Phenomenological Research* 51, 919–920.
Sen, A. (1982), 'Rights and agency', *Philosophy and Public Affairs,* Vol. 11, No. 1, 3–39.
Sosa, D. (1993), 'Consequences for consequentialism', *Mind*, Vol. 102, 101–122.

On consequentialism and special obligations:

Arneson, R. J. (2003), 'Consequentialism vs. special-ties partiality', *The Monist,* Vol. 86, 382–401.
Sen, A. (1982), 'Rights and agency', *Philosophy and Public Affairs,* Vol. 11, No. 1, 3–39.
Sidgwick, H. (1907), *The Methods of Ethics*, seventh edition, London: Macmillan, Book 4, Chapter 3.

CHAPTER NINE

THE WAY OUTCOMES ARE BROUGHT ABOUT

Utilitarians tell us to maximize well-being. It does not matter how well-being is maximized, whether it involves violating constraints or special duties. Even a non-classical utilitarian who assigns disvalue to violations must agree that it does not matter how these violations are brought about, for instance, whether the agent himself is committing them or whether he is just allowing other people to commit them.

In this chapter, I will look more closely at this controversial feature of utilitarianism. I will pay special attention to the so-called Trolley problem. This problem highlights three distinctions that are ignored by the utilitarian:

(1) Doing harm versus allowing harm.
(2) Intending harm versus foreseeing harm.
(3) Treating a person merely as a means versus treating a person as an end.

If these distinctions matter, then it matters a great deal how and why an outcome is brought about.

THE TROLLEY PROBLEM

This is how the story goes. Suppose that you are the driver of a trolley whose brakes are not working. In front of you on the left hand track there are five workmen who are repairing the track. They cannot see you. So, if you turn left you will run over them and kill them. You can turn right but again there will be someone working on the track. However, only one workman is standing there. So the choice is between killing five and killing one. What should you do? Most would think that it is at least permissible to turn right. Many would go further and say that we ought to turn right.[1]

There are many other cases that have exactly the same structure. Consider, for instance, a pilot who is going to crash with his plane and whose only option is to steer away from the city centre and crash in a less populated suburb. Again, it seems permissible, if not obligatory, to steer away from the city centre and cause less harm.

Now consider the Hospital case I introduced in the previous chapter. You are a surgeon facing a horrible dilemma. You have five patients who are dying. Two need one lung each, two need a kidney each, and the fifth needs a new heart. The time is almost up when a report is brought to you that a young man who has just come to your clinic for his yearly check-up has exactly the right blood type and is in excellent health. So you have a possible donor. All you need to do is to kill him and distribute his organs. Not surprisingly, he does not want to donate his organs. Should you nevertheless kill him? Assume that no one will know about it and no one will miss this young man. This is important. Of course, it would have disastrous consequences if people knew about your action. However, even when this qualification is added, most of us would say that you should not kill the patient.

The utilitarian, however, cannot judge these cases differently, since he thinks that the wrongness of killing is explained entirely in terms of the victim's loss of future well-being. In both cases, either the future well-being of one life is lost or the future well-being of five lives is lost. Since the loss of well-being to five people adds up to a greater loss, the utilitarian would have to say that it is right to kill one in order to save five. One could therefore argue that this shows that utilitarianism is false since it totally ignores *how* and *why* the deaths are brought about.

ACT-UTILITARIAN REPLIES

As I said before, the utilitarian seems to be forced to say that the doctor should cut up the healthy patient. Of course, remember that it is the classical utilitarian we are talking about here. A non-classical utilitarian does not have to say that the doctor ought to kill the patient, for he can say that it is much worse, in itself, for a patient to be killed and cut up than to be left to die. Thus, what the doctor is doing is intrinsically bad and, moreover, it is intrinsically worse than allowing five to die. This is perhaps a peculiar evaluation, and one that is in need of further defence, but it is still an option for a non-classical utilitarian. (A non-utilitarian consequentialist could simply say that what the doctor is doing is intrinsically bad, but not necessarily intrinsically bad for anybody.) Of course, he would still have to say that doctors are allowed to kill and cut up patients in order to minimize the total amount of similar killings, since badness ought to be minimized.

What could a classical utilitarian who accepts that killing the patient is permissible say in his defence? First, it is important that in the Hospital case no one will know about this killing, since, as we discussed in the previous chapter, if people knew about what happened, they would not dare to go to the hospital and that would cause a lot of harm. Furthermore, it must be certain that killing the patient is the only way to save the other patients. This means that the Hospital case is not as realistic as it first may seem. In real-life situations, there is always a significant risk that people will know about the doctor's actions, and also a risk that killing the patient will in fact not save the other patients. If the utilitarian is sensitive to risk, he would therefore say that *in real-life cases* it is normally wrong (or at least irrational) for doctors to cut up healthy patients.

Second, the utilitarian would urge us to be careful when we employ our moral intuitions in hypothetical cases. Our intuitions are adjusted to real-life cases where we cannot be certain about the outcomes of our actions. When we judge hypothetical cases we have a tendency to read into those cases features that are normally present in real-life cases. We should not expect our intuitions to be a reliable guide for highly idealized and far-fetched cases. As Hare reminds us, our 'intuitions are the product of [our] upbringings [. . .], and, however good these may have been [. . .], there is no guarantee at all that they will be appropriate to unusual cases'.[2]

Third, the utilitarian is not committed to the idea that there should be a policy among doctors to perform this kind of operation. As we discussed in the previous chapter, the consequences of having such a policy would be very bad, since doctors would sometimes make wrong judgements about the situation, and other people might get to know about their policy. Obviously, a utilitarian would not think that doctors should be taught in medical school to practice enforced donation. Indeed, as I pointed out in the previous chapter, it might be better that doctors do not even consider killing the healthy patient as an option.

Fourth, the utilitarian would in any case say that it is wrong to give up a strong aversion to this kind of killing. This kind of aversion seems to be the best attitude to have when you consider the alternatives. Just think of the consequences of having doctors around who are indifferent or even positively inclined towards killing healthy patients.

These replies will not impress everyone, since they all concede that in the Hospital case, with all idealizations in place, it is permissible for the doctor to cut up the healthy patient in order to save the other patients. But before we conclude that utilitarianism is obviously flawed, we need to know exactly why it is wrong to kill the healthy patient but not wrong to turn right and kill one person in the Trolley case. If it turns out that it is difficult to provide a plausible explanation of this intuitive difference, then this will give us reason to pause and reconsider our intuitive judgements about these cases. Remember that our intuitive judgements are only the starting point of the moral discussion. They cannot, without further arguments, be seen as the end point; we also need to see whether our intuitive judgements can be justified.

(1) DOING HARM VERSUS ALLOWING HARM

One attempt at justifying our different responses to the Trolley and Hospital cases is to claim that there is a moral difference between doing harm and allowing harm. This general idea can be made more precise in many different ways. Here is one simple version:

Doing/allowing-principle
It is always worse to do harm than to allow harm (given that the harm you allow is not morally disproportionate to the harm you actively bring about).

The worse option is understood as being impermissible and the better one permissible. The qualification about proportionality is important, since it would be absurd to say that you are not permitted to actively bring about some minor harm, a pin prick say, in order to save thousands of people from severe suffering.

However, the added qualification makes the principle vague, since it is not clear how to decide when an actively produced harm is morally disproportionate to a merely allowed harm. And this means that it no longer has clear implications for all possible cases. To fix this, we need some idea about how to weigh the harm done against the harm allowed. Would this amount to a collapse into utilitarianism or consequentialism? No, for it is still true that rightness in part depends on factors that are not about outcome values. If a doing and an allowing have exactly the same outcomes, it is still true that the doing is worse that the allowing.

The doing/allowing-principle might explain the difference between the Trolley case and the Hospital case. In the Hospital case, the doctor can do harm by killing one or allow harm by letting the five patients die. And the harm he actively brings about is a very great harm – taking someone's life – and the harm he allows are five deaths, not thousands of deaths, and thus the harm does not seem to be morally disproportionate to the harm allowed. Despite its vagueness, then, the doing/allowing principle should plausibly say:

Killing one is worse that allowing five to die.

In the Trolley case, there is no way to avoid doing harm, and therefore it seems plausible to say that we should simply minimize the harm done, that is:

Killing one is better than killing five.

So, the doing/allowing-principle seems to provide intuitively attractive prescriptions for the Trolley and the Hospital cases. But is this principle reasonable in other cases? Here is a counterexample (See Table 9.1). Suppose that someone has set up a devilish machine and hooked up six people to it. If anyone pushes the button on the machine, one person will die, if the button is not pushed, five other persons will die. Would anyone claim that, all other things being equal (including the agent's beliefs and intentions), not-pushing is

Table 9.1

Push	1 person dies
Not-push	5 other persons die

better than pushing and that it is therefore permissible not to push? This example suggests that the correct principle instead should be:

Doing/allowing principle*
It is *sometimes* worse to do harm than to allow harm, (given that the harm you allow is not morally disproportionate to the harm you actively bring about).

But then we need to know when and why it is worse. One worry here is that it is not the doing/allowing distinction that matters fundamentally. What matters fundamentally is rather the psychological make-up of the agent, his intentions, desires, and beliefs. Assume, for instance, that the reason you push the button is that you want the single person dead because you are after his money. This is a case where doing harm seems to be worse in one respect, (but perhaps not so bad as to make your action impermissible; note that five people will be saved if the button is pushed), but it seems to turn on the intention of the agent, not the fact that his action is a doing rather than an allowing.

One could even question whether the distinction between doings and allowings is well defined to start with. If I do not feed my children, do I do harm or merely allow harm? If you fail to turn up to the final rehearsal of a play with the foreseen result that the premiere has to be cancelled, do you do harm or merely allow harm? The problem is that some actions seem to be describable as both doings and allowings, and whether we would like to call something a doing rather than an allowing depends in part on our prior duties. For example, if a parent has a duty to feed his children, not giving them food seems to be a case of a doing: the parent is starving his children. If a complete stranger does not give my children food and it is assumed that he has no duty to do so, we would not call it a case of starving the children but only a case of allowing harm. But if the doing and allowing distinction presupposes prior duties, then, obviously, it cannot provide a fundamental explanation of our duties not to do harm.

So, the doing/allowing principle seems to have internal problems. In any case, further reflection shows that the principle is in fact unable to solve the Trolley problem. It gives the right results only if we make the questionable assumption that in the Trolley case we face a choice between two *doings*: doing more or less harm. But it seems more natural to say we can either *allow* the trolley to run over the workmen it is heading towards or *intervene* and make the trolley change tracks. To make this clearer, consider the following version of the Trolley case.

The bystander case

You have been strolling by the trolley track and you see the trolley coming. You know that the brakes do not work and that the driver has fainted. You can either do nothing and allow the trolley run over the five or you can throw the switch and turn the trolley, in which case it will run over one person. So here, the choice is between allowing five to die or killing one.[3]

The doing/allowing principle would not allow you to throw the switch in this case. Since we still think that you may throw the switch and kill one, we have not yet found a plausible explanation of why we should judge the Trolley case and the Hospital case differently.

(2) INTENDING HARM VERSUS FORESEEING HARM

The discussion so far suggests that it may be more important *why* an outcome is brought about than how it is brought about. One way to spell this idea out is to draw a distinction between intended effects and foreseen effects. You intend an outcome if you aim at it as an end or as a means to your ends, whereas you foresee an outcome if you know it will come about but do not aim at as an end or as a means to your ends.

Roughly, the idea is that it is morally worse to do good by intentionally doing something bad than to do good and only foreseeing that this will have bad effects. In slogan form, the ends do not justify the means. One way to make this idea more precise is this:

The double-effect doctrine
(1) You are *permitted* to intentionally realize a good end even if you *foresee* that this will have bad consequences (given that the badness of the foreseen effects is not morally disproportionate to the goodness of the end).
(2) You are *not permitted* to intentionally realize a good end *by* intentionally bringing about something bad (given that the badness of the means is not morally disproportionate to the goodness of the end).

Two comments are necessary here. First, one qualification that should be added is that we are not allowed to intentionally pursue a good end, foreseeing that it will have bad effect, if there is an alternative action that would realize the same good but which would not have any foreseen bad effects. We are only permitted to bring about foreseen bad effects if they are unavoidable effects of the intended good.

Second, the qualifications about proportionality are important, for without them we would have to say that you are allowed to pursue a moderately good end, foreseeing that it will cause horrible suffering for thousands of people. For instance, you would be allowed to raise the production of environmentally friendly cars in your factory, which we can assume is a moderately good thing, foreseeing that this will pollute a nearby river and, as a consequence, thousands of people will die from drinking the polluted water, which is much worse. Furthermore, without the qualification, you would not be allowed to intentionally bring about some minor suffering as a means to some highly valuable end, for instance, causing some minor suffering to an animal as a means to finding an effective cure for people (and animals) suffering from cancer.

The double-effect doctrine is a very popular doctrine and it is employed in medical ethics as well as the ethics of war. As I said in Chapter Two, one could use this principle to argue that terrorist attacks are worse than strategic bombings, since a terrorist intends the deaths of the civilians, whereas a strategic bomber merely foresees that by destroying an ammunition factory he will kill civilians living nearby. (Whether this argument is successful in justifying real-life cases of strategic bombing is another question. Remember that strategic bombing is justified only if there is no other option available that would not have the bad side effects.)

After these preliminaries, let us turn to the main question: Can the double-effect doctrine solve the Trolley problem? Consider the Bystander case again. The bystander intends to save the five workmen by throwing the switch. But he does not intend to kill the person on the right hand track. His death is not the ultimate end of his action, neither is it a means to his end. The bystander's plan would be successful even if the person on the track were able to leave the track. He would not need to drag him back to the track and kill him in order to realize his plan. So his death is just something the bystander foresees.

What is going on in the Hospital case is quite different. The doctor intends to save the five patients *by* killing one patient. The healthy patient's death is intended, not just foreseen. It is by killing the patient the doctor will be able to implement his plan to save the five patients. If the patient left the hospital, he would not be able to implement his plan.

Now, one obvious complication is that the doctor could say that he is not really intending the death of the healthy patient. He only intends to use his organs. Of course, he does realize that this will inevitably lead to the patient's death, but that is a foreseen effect, not an intended effect. The doctor would be greatly relieved if he could somehow use the patient's organs without killing him. To make this point clearer, suppose that the doctor does not plan to kill the patient first and then when he is dead take out his organs. Instead, his plan is to keep the patient alive *while* he is taking out the organs. Only once the organs have been taken out will he shut off the life-support. In this case, it seems more difficult to insist that the doctor is aiming at the death of the patient as a means to use his organs.

This may sound like a clever trick. How could the doctor sincerely claim that he is not intending the patient's death? There is no way the doctor can use his organs without killing him. This response assumes something like the following principle:

Closeness principle
If you intend A as means to a certain end, and B is 'sufficiently close' to A, then you also intend B as a means to this end.

What does 'sufficiently close' mean? One option is to understand 'B is sufficiently close to A' as 'B is logically entailed by A'. This will not do, since using the patient's organs does not logically entail his death. It is logically possible for the patient to survive this operation – it is logically possible that he is saved by an angel, for instance.

Another option is to understand 'B is sufficiently close to A' as 'B is caused by A'. It is true that using the patient's organs will cause the person to die. But if this is the right criterion, killing the single person on the right track in the Bystander case would also count as part of the means, since throwing the switch will cause the person to die.

Despite these failures, we might still want to say that the death of the patient just *feels* close to the act of using his organs. But this would be to admit defeat, since no analysis is provided. I am not saying that these are the only possibilities. I just want to point out that finding a plausible criterion that shows that the doctor is intending the death rather than foreseeing the death is more difficult than one might first think.

No matter how we make the concept of intended consequences more precise, the double-effect doctrine gives an inadequate treatment of the problem, as the following version of the Trolley problem shows.

The Loop case

There is a big heavy man on the right-hand track and the track loops back to the five on the left-hand track. So, if you throw the switch, the trolley will kill the single man, but since he is so big and heavy he will actually stop the trolley from going round and killing the five. The five on the other track would also stop the trolley (otherwise the big man would be doomed and the moral problem less difficult).[4] Even in this case, many people would say that it is permissible to throw the switch. But here you seem to intend the trolley to run over the big man. It is part of your plan to stop the trolley by bumping into the big man. Now the problem is that, since there is no way you can avoid killing the man if you run over him, the relation between running over him and killing him seems to be as close as the relation between using the patient's organs and killing him. So, if you think that the doctor is saving five by intentionally killing one, you have to say that in the Loop case you are also saving five by intentionally killing one. But still, many would want to say that it is permissible to throw the switch but not permissible to use the patient's organs. Thus the double-effect doctrine does not give us a plausible explanation of why the Trolley and the Hospital case should be judged differently.

(3) TREATING PEOPLE MERELY AS MEANS/TREATING PEOPLE AS ENDS

The final deontological proposal I will discuss is Kantian in spirit, indeed it could be seen as an interpretation of Kant's own Humanity principle, which we briefly introduced in Chapter Three. The proposal says that it is wrong to treat people merely as a means and right to treat them as ends. 'Merely' is an important qualification here, since, as I pointed out in Chapter Three, in many social interactions we do make use of other people. Just think about your interactions with shopkeepers, taxi drivers, and mechanics. You do treat these people and their services as a means to your ends; it is just that you do not treat them merely as a means. If we apply this principle to the Loop case, we could say that when we plan to run into the big man we are treating him as a means to saving the five, but we are not treating him *merely* as a means. We would not be willing to push him back on the track if he tried to escape. That would be treating him merely as a means. Since we do think that he is an end and his death a serious loss, we are not treating him as a *mere* means when we run into him in order to save five. So, we seem justified in killing him. In contrast, in the Hospital case, the doctor is just using the patient as a resource for harvesting useful organs, and that is wrong.

The problem here is that the notion of treating someone merely as a means is not easy to define. It is especially difficult to find a plausible definition that would show that the doctor does not treat his patient as an end if he kills him and uses his organs to save the other patients. Of course, no one can deny that the doctor is using the patient as a means. But even if the doctor is a utilitarian, he will not think that the patient is a *mere tool* to be used at his own discretion. The patient is an end in the sense that his welfare matters as much as anybody else's. Killing him is therefore a serious loss, but allowing five to die is an even greater loss. The challenge here is therefore to show that the utilitarian doctor is *merely* using the patient as a means. One option would be to say that:

> You treat someone merely as a means if and only if you do something to this person without her consent.

Since the doctor is killing the agent without his consent, he is acting wrongly. But on this interpretation of the Kantian principle, you are not allowed to kill the big person in the Loop case either, for we can assume that he does not consent to be killed. Another option is to say:

> You treat someone merely as a means if and only if you do not give her any moral significance.

Of course, the deontologist cannot then define giving moral significance to a person as merely giving weight to his well-being, because then the utilitarian doctor could not be faulted for killing the healthy patient. The deontologists need a more demanding notion of moral significance. Could the notion of inviolability, introduced in the previous chapter, fit the bill?

This is doubtful. Remember that inviolability is a matter of what can permissibly be *done* to people. Both the big man in the Loop case and the healthy patient in the Hospital case are victims of doings. If we run into the big man in the Loop case, we do something to him without his consent. If we cut up the healthy patient, we do something to him without his consent. If every person is inviolable, how can we permissibly run into the big man and kill him but not permissibly use the patient's organs?

Remember also that utilitarians do assign some degree of inviolability to persons: no one can be permissibly harmed in order to prevent a lesser amount of harm to others. So, even on this understanding of moral significance, the utilitarian doctor who sacrifices the healthy patient is giving his patient some moral significance.

The deontologist would of course object that to treat people as ends we need to give them a higher degree of inviolability. The problem is that a higher degree of inviolability comes at the price of a lower degree of *saveability*. For instance, if no one could be permissibly killed and have their organs taken out to save five others, then *everyone's* saveability would be diminished, for it would now be true that no one could be permissibly saved by this route. The Trolley case seems thus to illustrate a difficult conflict between two important aspects of moral significance: inviolability and saveability. The deontologist stresses the inviolability aspect, whereas the utilitarian stresses the saveability aspect. Who is right? Well, the answer seems to depend crucially on whether there is a moral distinction between what is done to people and what is allowed to happen to people, but, as we have seen, this distinction is not easy to defend.

CONCLUDING REMARKS

The Trolley problem is a good illustration of how difficult it is to come up with a plausible explanation of why intuitively wrong actions are wrong. The utilitarian does provide a clear explanation of why it is right to kill one to save five, an explanation that applies equally well in the Trolley case and the Hospital case. Of course, we might not like this explanation because it condones the doctor's killing the patient in order to save the five. The grim choice seems to be between an unclear or implausible deontological explanation that gives the intuitively right prescriptions and a clear utilitarian explanation that gives the intuitively wrong prescriptions.

To decide the matter we need to know how much we can trust our moral intuitions. Some recent empirical research suggests that those of us who judge that the doctor is justified to cut up the healthy patient to save others are driven by controlled cognitive processes, often associated with rational thinking, whereas those of us who judge his action impermissible are driven by automatic, intuitive emotional responses. Some think that this shows that the non-utilitarian intuitions are less trustworthy, since they are more based on automatic gut feelings than detached rational thinking, but things are not so simple.[5] For instance, we know from history that being driven by controlled cognitive processes does not prevent one from doing horrible things without any second thoughts. Indeed, the lack of emotional responses can be a sign of a morally corrupt mind.

SUGGESTED READING

On acts and omissions:

Foot, P. (1978), 'The problem of abortion and the doctrine of double effect', in her *Virtues and Vices*, Berkeley, CA: University of California Press.

Glover, J. (1977), *Causing Deaths and Saving Lives*, London: Penguin, Chapter 7.

Kagan, S. (1989), *The Limits of Morality*, Oxford: Oxford University Press, Chapter 3.

Rachels, J. (1994), 'Active and passive euthanasia', in Steinbock, B. and Norcross, A., (eds.), *Killing and Letting Die*, New York: Fordham University Press.

On intended effects and foreseen effects:

Foot, P. (1978), 'The problem of abortion and the doctrine of double effect', in her *Virtues and Vices*, Berkeley, CA: University of California Press.

Glover, J. (1977), *Causing Deaths and Saving Lives*, London: Penguin, Chapter 6.

Kagan, S. (1989), *The Limits of Morality*, Oxford: Oxford University Press, Chapter 4.

On the Trolley problem:

Davis, N. A. (1994), 'The priority of avoiding harm', in Steinbock, B. and Norcross A., (eds.), *Killing and Letting Die*, New York: Fordham University Press, 298–354.

Foot, P. (1978), 'The problem of abortion and the doctrine of double effect', in her *Virtues and Vices*, Berkeley, CA: University of California Press.
Thomson, J. J. (1986), 'The Trolley problem', in Patent, W. A., (ed.), *Rights, Restitution and Risk: Essays in Moral Theory*, Cambridge, MA: Harvard University Press, 94–116.

On saveability:

Kamm, F. (2007), *Intricate Ethics*, Oxford: Oxford University Press, 254–255.
Otsuka, M. (1997), 'Kamm on the morality of killing', *Ethics*, Vol. 108, 197–207.

On treating someone as an end/merely as a means:

O'Neill, O. (1989), *Constructions of Reason*, Cambridge: Cambridge University Press. Chapter 6.
Scanlon, T. M. (2008), *Permissibility, Meaning, Blame*, Belknap Press of Cambridge, MA: Harvard University Press, Chapter 3.

CHAPTER TEN

THE PLACE OF RULES IN UTILITARIANISM

We have shown that classical utilitarianism runs counter to many of our dearest common-sense moral views. It is both too demanding and too permissive. It is too demanding, since it sometimes requires agents to make heroic sacrifices for the sake of others; it is too permissive, since it accepts no constraints or special duties. A particularly vivid illustration of the utilitarian laxness about constraints was brought up in the last chapter. Utilitarianism would demand a doctor to kill an innocent person, cut him up, and distribute his organs in order to save five other people.

Now, rule-utilitarians will claim that these problems do not refute utilitarianism as such, only *act*-utilitarianism. As they see it, act-utilitarianism is too act-oriented, for it counts only the consequences of individual actions. We should instead judge actions by the consequences of the rules under which they fall. If we do this, we will avoid the problems that plague act-utilitarianism. For instance, even if the doctor's action of killing the patient would maximize total well-being, it is doubtful that total well-being would be maximized if every doctor accepted a rule that permitted them to cut up one healthy patient in order to save five.

The question I shall discuss in this chapter is whether rule-utilitarianism is superior to act-utilitarianism. In particular, I shall ask whether rule-utilitarianism can accommodate constraints, as well as special duties and options, without at the same time betraying the spirit of utilitarianism. In the last section I will turn to act-utilitarianism and see whether there is any place left for rules in this theory.

RULE UTILITARIANISM

Both rule- and act-utilitarianism are primarily interested in determining the rightness of individual actions. They also agree that outcome values fully determine rightness. But they disagree about which outcomes are relevant. Act-utilitarianism judges actions directly by their consequences, whereas rule-utilitarianism judges actions indirectly by the consequences of the rules under which the actions fall.

The bare bones of a rule-utilitarian theory can be presented as follows:

(1) An action is right if and only if it falls under the best system of rules.
(2) A system of rules is best if and only if it has better consequences than any other system of rules.
(3) One system of rules has better consequences than another if and only if the former would bring about a greater total amount of well-being than the latter.

(1) and (2) define rule-consequentialism. It is only if we add (3) that we get rule-utilitarianism. A rule-consequentialist can of course deny (3) and instead adopt some non-utilitarian evaluation of the outcomes of rules.

What does it mean to say that a system of rules has consequences? Strictly speaking, no rule can just by itself have consequences. For instance, it does not make sense to ask what consequences 'Do not lie' would have. But it does make sense to ask what would happen if everyone *accepted* the rule 'Do not lie'. It also makes sense to ask what would happen if everyone *followed* this rule. Since you can accept a rule without always conforming to it – you may be weak willed, swayed by temptations, or likely to misapply the rule because of lack of information – the rule-utilitarian must decide whether to formulate his theory in terms of the consequences of everyone accepting a rule or the consequences of everyone conforming to a rule. The choice is between, what I shall call, *the acceptance version* and *the conformity version* of rule-utilitarianism. Both versions agree that 'What will happen if I lie?' is the wrong question to ask. But they differ in what they think is the right question to ask. Whereas the acceptance version thinks the right question is 'What would happen if everyone *accepted* a rule that says it is fine to lie in this situation?', the conformity version thinks it is 'What would happen if everybody *followed* a rule that says it is fine to lie in this situation?'

THE COLLAPSE ARGUMENT

It may be tempting to think that rule-utilitarianism is not a serious alternative to act-utilitariansm, for how could the act-utilitarian rule 'Maximize total-well-being' fail to have the best consequences? But it is clear that *accepting* the act-utilitarian rule will not have the best consequences. As noted in Chapter Six, ordinary humans do not have the motivation and information necessary to apply the rule correctly in all cases. So, the acceptance version of rule-utilitarianism is definitely a serious alternative to act-utilitarianism.

What about the conformity version? There is a popular argument that aims to show that this version of rule-utilitarianism gives exactly the same prescriptions as act-utilitarianism. This collapse argument, as it is often called, starts by considering some simple rule such as 'Do not lie'. Is there a rule that would have better consequences if everyone followed it? Surely there is. Just think of a case in which I ask you if I look fat in my new jeans. If you tell me the truth, you will cause some minor harm to me. So, in this kind of situation, it would surely have better consequences, if everyone followed a rule such as 'Do not lie except when you can avoid causing some minor embarrassment to a person by lying to him'. Have we now found the best rule? No, because we could think about other cases where more harm is at stake, for instance, a case where an enemy soldier, bent on killing your friend, asks for his whereabouts. To tell the truth in this kind of situation would mean that a person is killed. So, an even better rule is 'Do not lie except when you can avoid causing some minor embarrassment to a person or save a life by lying.' But this game can be repeated by adding more exception clauses until we reach the rule 'Do not lie except when you can maximize total well-being by lying'. This reasoning can be generalized. For any action A, following the rule 'Do not do A except when doing A will maximize total well-being' will have better consequences than following the rule 'Do not do A'. So we seem to have shown that the rule that would have the best consequences, if generally followed, is simply 'Maximize total well-being'. But this means that the conformity version of rule-utilitarianism will always give the same prescriptions as act-utilitarianism.

This reasoning is flawed, however. Here is a simple counter-example.[1] Suppose that each of us has two options: go to The King's Arms, a very popular pub, or go to The Oz, a less exciting pub. Suppose, further, that we act independently of each other. We cannot communicate with each other before we decide where to go (we have no mobile phones, for instance). If we both go to The Oz, we will have fun but not great fun (overall well-being 6). If we both go to the more exciting pub The King's Arms, we will both have a great time (overall well-being 10). If we go to different places, we will miss out on the fun since we will not be together (overall well-being 0). See Table 10.1 which illustrates the situation.

Suppose that for some reason we both end up going to The Oz. (Perhaps we mistakenly think that this would be most fun for us.) Would each of us then act rightly according to act-utilitarianism? Surprisingly, the answer is yes. To see this, consider first how things look from my perspective. Since you are in fact going to The Oz, I am facing the choice as shown in Table 10.2. Since it is better if I go to The Oz (value 6) than if I go to The King's Arms (value 0), I ought to go to The Oz. Now, consider how things look from your perspective. Since I will in fact go to The Oz, you are facing the choice as shown in Table 10.3. Since it is better if you go to The Oz (value 6) than if you go to The King's Arms (value 0), you ought to go to The Oz. So, the surprising conclusion is that in a situation where we both go to The Oz, we each act rightly according to act-utilitarianism.

Table 10.1

	You go to The King's Arms	You go to The Oz
I go to The King's Arms	10	0
I go to The Oz	0	6

Table 10.2

I go to The King's Arms	0
I go to The Oz	6

Table 10.3

You go to The King's Arms	You go to The Oz
0	6

Table 10.4

Rules	Consequences, if followed
'We go to The King's Arms'	Value 10
'We go to The Oz'	Value 6
'I go to The King's Arms, you go to The Oz'	Value 0
'You go to The King's Arms, I go to The Oz'	Value 0

What would the conformity version of rule-utilitarianism tell us to do? To answer this we need to decide which rule would have the best consequences *if we followed it*. Table 10.4 shows the relevant rules and their respective consequences, if followed. The best rule is therefore 'Go to The King's Arms'. So, each of us ought to go to The King's Arms, and this holds no matter what the other person will in fact do.

This example shows that the collapse argument is mistaken. It is easy to make this mistake, however, since it is tempting to think that if all agents act in accordance with act-utilitarianism, *they* will together produce the best consequences *they* can together produce. But what is true is only that if all satisfy act-utilitarianism, *each* agent will produce the best consequences *he* can produce (given the behaviour of other agents). The example above shows that it is possible that each agent does the best he can and yet it is not true that the agents jointly do the best they can.

COMPLIANCE VERSUS ACCEPTANCE

As we have seen, both the acceptance version and the conformity version are serious alternatives to act-utilitarianism. One possible reason to choose the acceptance version is that it seems to have an easier time accommodating constraints, special duties, and options.

For instance, if everyone *followed* the rule 'kill one patient in order to save five when no one will know about it' the consequences would be good overall. Each doctor is saving five at the cost of one life but there will be no bad side effects. So, the conformity version must say that this rule has something going for it. If, in contrast, everyone *accepted* this rule, the consequences are not likely to be good overall, because doctors will make mistakes or lack sufficient motivation and thus not always follow the rule. So, the acceptance version would not think highly of this rule.

Since the acceptance version is a more clear-cut alternative to act-utilitarianism, I will assume it in the following. Other reasons to favour the acceptance version will be highlighted later when we consider objections to rule-utilitarianism.

ADVANTAGES OF RULE-UTILITARIANISM

On the face of it, rule-utilitarianism has some clear advantages over act-utilitarianism:

(1) It ties in with our moral practice of testing moral judgements by putting them through a *universalization* test. If your friend tells you that it is fine for him to evade taxes or cheat in exams because his deviation from generally upheld norms will not cause any bad consequences, your reaction is likely to be 'What if everyone thought it would be OK to do that?' The rule-utilitarian thinks this is the right question to ask and adds that the answer should be stated in terms of the consequences of everyone's thinking that it is OK to perform that action.

(2) Rule-utilitarianism seems also able to avoid the charge of being too demanding. A rule that prohibits people to pursue their innocent projects at the expense of overall well-being would not have good consequences if it was generally accepted. Bad consequences will emerge if people accept a theory that demands too much of them. For instance, they will often fail to live up to their high standards and this failure will lower their morale. The best rule will therefore be a rule that gives agents some options.

(3) The charge of being too permissive can also be avoided. The rule-utilitarian would argue that the best system of rules will incorporate important constraints. For instance, the best system of rules

will not permit doctors to cut up healthy patients and distribute their organs to save others, because if doctors thought that this was OK, disastrous consequences would follow.

Similarly, if people thought it was OK to break a promise, lie, or cheat for the sake of some minor benefit, people would lose trust in each other. So, the best system of rules will contain some prohibitions against breaking promises, lying, and cheating for minor gains.

Special obligations also seem to have a place in the best rule, since we are often in a better position to benefit our nearest and dearest. Also, if we all went around feeling the same responsibility for every person our sense of responsibility would get diluted.

OBJECTIONS TO RULE-UTILITARIANISM

Poor guide to action

One may think that rule-utilitarianism is a more user-friendly theory than act-utilitarianism because it may seem easier to know what one ought to do according to rule-utilitarianism. Since the best system of rules will to a large extent coincide with common sense, rule-utilitarianism will tell you not to cheat, lie, and break promises. And these duties are pretty user-friendly: it is normally quite easy to know how to comply with them. However, this assumes that we have already established that the best system of rules will include these common-sense duties. But this assumes a lot. Remember that the best system is defined as the system that would have the best consequences if *everyone* accepted it. But 'everyone' includes not just us living here and now but also future people. Even if we can be reasonably certain that a system including duties from our current conventional morality would have the best consequences, if *we* accepted it, we cannot be certain that this system would also have the best consequences, if it were accepted not just by us but by *all future generations*. Who knows how the future of humanity will develop and what capacities future people will have? This means that the rule-utilitarian will also have to face the knowledge problem we discussed in Chapter Six. I cannot easily know what I ought to do, since I cannot easily know what is the best system of rules for all present and future generations.

The rule-utilitarian can of course redefine his theory in terms of the *expected* value of accepting a system of rules. But, as noted in Chapter Six, the act-utilitarian can redefine his theory in terms of the expected value of individual acts. So, rule-utilitarianism does not seem to have an advantage over act-utilitarianism with respect to usability.

Partial compliance

A standard objection to rule-utilitarianism is that it seems to suffer from the same wrong-headed idealism we find in the naive pacifist: 'If everyone accepted my pacifist principles, there would be no wars and no need to take up arms. Therefore, I should not take up arms.' This is wrong-headed, since we have to decide what to do in an imperfect world. We know that we will have to interact with immoral agents who are not interested in doing right and also with moral agents who will often fail to live up to their moral standards. When the rule-utilitarian asks what would happen if everyone accepted a moral rule, he rules out the possibility of dealing with people who do not accept any moral rules. For instance, if everyone fully accepted rules forbidding harming the innocent, stealing, promise breaking, and lying, there would be little or no need for rules about punishing the perpetrators and compensating their victims. But surely that does not show that there is no justification for punishments and compensations in the real world. The root of the problem is that deciding what to do on the basis of what would happen if everyone accepted certain rules is in effect to imagine out of existence people who do not accept moral rules.

In reply, the rule-utilitarian could point out that if the theory is formulated in terms of acceptance rather than compliance, there is still some room left for dealing with people who accept rules but fail to act on them. This is only a partial response, of course, since we still need to deal with people who do not accept any moral rules. To deal with these people, the theory has to be revised so that it does not ask for full acceptance. Rather, as Brad Hooker suggests, we should ask what would happen if an *overwhelming* majority accepted a certain rule.[2] More exactly:

An act is wrong if and only if it is prohibited by a system of rules the acceptance of which by the overwhelming majority of all people would bring about the greatest total well-being.

This revised theory will make it possible to deal with a minority of amoral people who do not accept any moral rules. Note, however, that this response will make rule-utilitarianism vague, since it is not clear which exact percentage of acceptance we should go for. Hooker suggests 90 per cent, but admits that this is somewhat arbitrary.[3] Perhaps this imprecision is something we can live with, but it should be noted that it makes rule-utilitarianism more difficult to apply.

Disaster prevention

Another related objection to rule-utilitarianism is that acting according to the best rule may lead to a disaster in the real situation. Suppose that all that is needed to prevent two children from starving to death is the donation of 10 pounds, and that you and I can easily donate 5 pounds each. Suppose further that I will in fact donate my share, but you will not. Is it then true that I Should still donate my share of 5 pounds and smugly think that I did my fair share, when in fact the children are left to die and I could easily have saved them by donating 10 pounds?

In reply, the rule-utilitarian would question whether the best rule for this kind of situation will be 'give 5 pounds each to save the child'. A better rule seems to be 'give 5 pounds each to save the child, except when one of us will fail to donate, in which case give 10 pounds'. More generally, the rule-utilitarian could argue that the best system of rules will contain disaster prevention rules of something like the form 'Do your fair share, except when doing your fair share leads to a disaster because of others' failure to comply, and you can without great sacrifice do something else instead and thereby prevent the disaster.' This does not mean that we are back to the stringent rules of act-utilitarianism, for act-utilitarians will tell us to make up for others' moral failures even if only *slightly* more well-being will be gained that way.

Of course, it is not clear exactly what should count as a disaster in the rule-utilitarian theory – a lost life, a lost limb, excruciating pain, depression? So, again, we would have to put up with some imprecision in the moral theory and accept that it is less clear how it should be applied.

Furthermore, following qualified rules of this kind can add up to a great sacrifice over time. If I am unlucky and repeatedly meet with non-compliance from others, my constantly making up for the moral failures of others will add up to a significant cost to me.

NO BEST SYSTEM OF RULES

The formulations of rule-utilitarianism we have considered so far all state that we should do what is prescribed by *the* best system of rules. But this implicitly assumes that there will always be one unique best system of rules. This is questionable. Consider two systems of rules that differ only in one respect: one system tells us to drive on the left, the other, to drive on the right. It is not implausible to fill in the details so that these systems are equally good but better than all other relevant rule systems. In this case, rule-utilitarianism does not tell you whether to drive on the left or on the right. One might think that when there is such a tie, we could just say that either action is permissible. But that would be problematic, since it would then permit you to drive on the right at the same time as it permits me to drive on the left.

Here is another example, recently given by Brad Hooker:

> Imagine that contraceptive pills are available for both males and females. Now imagine two possible rules about contraception. One says it is primarily the male's responsibility. The other says it is primarily the female's responsibility. Suppose these two rules have equal expected value. Now, a moral theory had better not be such that two people could be fully following the theory and nei-ther of them using contraception during intercourse with one another (unless of course they both want her to become pregnant). But that is just what would happen if he followed the rule 'contra-ception is primarily the female's responsibility' and she followed the rule 'contraception is primarily the male's responsibility'.[4]

Hooker has suggested that in cases of ties like this, we should follow the system of rules that comes closest to conventional morality.[5] But this is a problematic suggestion for several reasons. First, it assumes that whenever we have a tie, one system of rules is closer to conventional morality than the other. But this seems unwarranted, especially if we consider the rules that prescribe things for situations that conventional morality has no clear view on. Hooker's own example seems to be a case in point. Moreover, new technological advances, such as cloning and artificial insemination, can force us to make difficult ethical decisions without having any clear guidance from common-sense morality.

Second, this response also assumes that there is one unique conventional morality we can use as a point of comparison. But moral conventions differ from one place to another and from one culture to another. If there are several moral conventions in play at the time of decision, which one should we chose as the reference point? The majority view? What if there is no clear majority?

Finally, by invoking conventional morality as a tiebreaker the rule-utilitarian can no longer claim that nothing but outcome-values matter for rightness. When two systems of rules are tied in terms of outcome-values, other factors supplemented by conventional morality will break the tie. This qualification therefore amounts to a small, but still significant, departure from a purely consequentialist framework.

CLOSER TO COMMON SENSE?

Rule-utilitarians often pride themselves of offering a theory that in many ways comes closer to common-sense morality. For instance, they point out that it ties in with our moral practice of judging actions by asking 'What would happen if everyone felt free to do that?' They also point out that rule-utilitarianism often coincides with common-sense morality. The best rule, they believe, will include general prohibitions against lying, cheating, breaking promises, and killing the innocent.

It should be stressed, however, that lurking behind this agreement between rule-utilitarianism and common-sense morality is a more fundamental disagreement about what makes actions right or wrong. For instance, what makes it wrong to break a certain promise according to the rule-utilitarian is the fact that this action is forbidden by a system of rules whose general acceptance would bring about the greatest total of well-being. Common-sense, in contrast, would not invoke the consequences of rules in the explanation of why promise breaking is wrong. Instead, what makes it wrong is something about you and the person you made a promise to, perhaps simply the fact that you made a promise to him. Similarly, according to common sense, the fundamental reason why you ought not to steal from the grocer is not that this kind of action would have bad consequences if generally accepted, but something about what you did to the grocer, perhaps the fact that you violated his property rights.

In reply, the rule-utilitarian could argue that, if common-sense morality insists that different duties have different duty-makers, we will end up with 'a heap of unconnected duties', to use Hooker's apt phrase. Each duty has its own fundamental explanation and there is no unifying explanation of our duties. Rule-utilitarianism, in contrast, could accept the conventional duties but also provide a unifying explanation of them. Since a unifying account is preferable, all other things being equal, rule-utilitarianism is superior to common-sense morality.

One crucial question here is of course whether the rule-utilitarian account is the best unifying account on offer. Kantianism, virtue ethics, and act-utilitarianism also provide unifying accounts. Another question is whether the rule-utilitarian account is true to the spirit of utilitarianism, a question to which I now turn.

DO RULE-UTILITARIANS CARE TOO LITTLE ABOUT WELL-BEING?

No one denies that it would be wrong for me to kick my cat for the sheer fun of it. But why is it wrong? Well, the most straightforward answer is to say that it is wrong at least in part because I cause needless suffering to the cat. This is the answer that act-utilitarianism would give, but common-sense morality would agree because it does not deny that sometimes an action is wrong in part because of its consequences. Both act-utilitarianism and common-sense morality would also agree that what makes it wrong for me to deliberately stamp on your toes is, at least in part, the fact that it will cause you severe pain.

However, the rule-utilitarian cannot accept these explanations. For him, these acts are wrong because they are forbidden by a system of rules that would have optimal consequences, if generally accepted. So, both common sense and act-utilitarianism will accuse rule-utilitarianism of misidentifying the wrong-makers of many actions.

Furthermore, act-utilitarians would accept that if an action would make someone better off without making anyone worse off, then that is a reason to perform it. Common-sense morality would agree, at least if the action neither violates any constraints, nor causes any unfair inequality, nor benefits people who do not deserve to be benefited. Again, the rule-utilitarian would disagree. All fundamental reasons must be phrased in terms of the consequences of the general acceptance of rules.

This means that in one crucial respect the rule-utilitarian account of rightness and wrongness is further away from common-sense morality than the act-utilitarian account. It also means that it is questionable whether rule-utilitarians are true to the spirit of utilitarianism, for, arguably, a true utilitarian should care directly and fundamentally about how his actions affect the well-being of others.

THE PLACE OF RULES IN ACT-UTILITARIANISM

Act-utilitarians think that it is misguided to judge actions by the consequences of rules. Does this mean that they have no place for rules in their theory then? No.

First, as I pointed out in earlier chapters, the act-utilitarian theory is a poor decision method. It is very time-consuming, since it requires complex calculations. Indeed, act-utilitarianism would tell us not to use it as a decision method because in many cases this will only have bad consequences. Since we cannot get by without some kind of decision method, we need to adopt some non-utilitarian decision method. Many act-utilitarians would argue that sticking to conventional rules will do fine in most cases. No better result would be gained by abandoning well-entrenched rules that prohibit lying, cheating, breaking promises, and harming the innocent.

This is not to put act-utilitarianism out of business, for it is still true that the act-utilitarian criterion is what ultimately decides which decision method we should adopt. As Mill points out, 'To inform a traveller respecting the place of his ultimate destination is not to forbid the use of landmarks and direction-posts on the way. The proposition that happiness is the end and aim of morality, does not mean that no road ought to be laid down to that goal, or that persons going thither should not be advised to take one direction rather than another.'[6] Nor is it to encourage a shallow commitment to common-sense duties. As noted in Chapter Seven, we can hardly expect to reap the good consequences of accepting conventional rules if we do not also *feel* constrained by them. The best consequences will come about only if we feel a strong aversion towards lying, cheating, breaking promises, and killing the innocent.

Second, rules will also play a crucial role in teaching children. The act-utilitarian would not argue with parents who teach their children not to lie, cheat, and harm other children. For it is difficult to see what could be a better alternative. Obviously, it would be futile to tell your 3-year-old that he ought to maximize overall well-being, because he can hardly understand what that means, nor can we expect him to suc-ceed if he did understand the rule and tried to follow it. The rules we teach our children have to be kept simple and manageable. When they grow older and become more sensitive to the complexities of moral life we can start adjusting the rules by introducing exception clauses. The utilitarian theory can then be introduced as a unifying explana-tion of why it is sometimes permissible to lie, cheat, or harm others. In fact, recent empirical research suggests that proto-utilitarian reasoning is accessible to very young children.[7] Young children tend to think that physical attacks, such as pulling hair and pushing, are wrong because it hurts the victim. They also tend to think that these actions would be wrong even if some authority, such as a parent or a teacher, gave them permission to perform these actions. In contrast, actions such as chew-ing gum in class and talking out of turn are thought to be less wrong and viewed as highly dependent on authority.

Third, as we grow up we need to take more charge of our own character development. We need to make decisions about which character traits to maintain, which to develop, and which to suppress. For these character-forming decisions, act-utilitarians will think that common-sense rules will be a good starting point. For instance, they would not take issue with our normal aspirations to become more charitable, honest, and benevolent. To aim to be less charitable, hon-est, and benevolent would only result in less total well-being.

Of course, we cannot just take for granted that whatever rules we have learned at mother's knee will in fact be the best ones for us to act on. For one thing, at some mother's knees you learn racist and sexist rules. But even if we consider more attractive moral conventions, it is likely that act-utilitarianism would ask us to be much more other-regarding, especially since so many people are in dire need of help. Act-utilitarianism would still be a demanding guide for character development. However, as we pointed out in Chapter Seven, this does not mean that we should grudgingly do our very best for others. Rather, we should change ourselves so that we take more pleasure in other-regarding projects.

Exactly how demanding the act-utilitarian theory will be is a contested issue among act-utilitarians. Some, *the conservatives*, like Sidgwick, Mill, and Hare, think that we can to a large extent rely on common-sense rules. These rules have been tested by past generations and we know therefore that following them is likely to maximize total well-being in the long-run. Act-utilitarianism will only be wheeled in when there is a conflict between conventional rules. Others, *the radicals*, like Peter Singer and Peter Unger, think we must make some radical changes to our common-sense views.[8] We need to radically reconsider the way we treat animals, for instance. Since animal well-being counts as much as human well-being – to deny it would be a form of speciecism akin to racism – we must stop using animals in medical testing and food farming. We must also reconsider the way we view international aid. The affluent people should stop thinking that they are morally justified in not sending aid to starving and ill people in developing countries. They have to consider donating much of their surplus to the needy (Singer suggests that 10 per cent of our income may be a useful approximation.[9])

I will not try to decide who is right. This is a complex question that hangs on difficult psychological, economical, and political issues. Suffice it to say that the more pessimistic your view is on our ability to improve our characters and successfully act in accordance with them, the more conservative your act-utilitarian theory will be in practice.

CONCLUDING REMARKS

Rule-utilitarianism shows an indirect concern for people's well-being. This indirect concern could be seen as an advantage, since it enables rule-utilitarianism to embrace a version of the popular universalization test, namely, 'How would people's well-being be affected, if everyone followed or accepted the rule under which your action falls?' This indirect concern also makes for a theory that to a large extent agrees with common-sense morality about which actions are right. However, the rule-utilitarian explanation of why these actions are right will not please common-sense morality. For example, it is an explanation that seems to reflect an all too indirect concern for the well-being of people and animals. When I kick my cat, the important question is not, 'What would happen if everyone did something similar to their cats?'; the relevant question is simply, 'How will this affect my cat?'. In this sense, rule-utilitarians depart from both common-sense morality and the core of classical utilitarianism.

SUGGESTED READING

On rule-utilitarianism:

Brandt, R. B. (1992), *Morality, Utilitarianism, and Rights*, Cambridge: Cambridge University Press, Chapters 7–8.

Brandt, R. B. (1996), *Facts , Value, and Morality*, New York: Cambridge University Press.

Hooker, B. (2000), *Ideal Code, Real World*, Oxford: Oxford University Press.

Hooker, Mason, and Miller, (eds.), (2000), *Morality, Rules, and Consequentialism*, Edinburgh: Edinburgh University Press.

Regan, D. (1980), *Utilitarianism and Co-operation*, Oxford: Clarendon Press, Chapters 5–6.

On the collapse argument:

Lyons, D. (1965), *Forms and Limits of Utilitarianism*, Oxford: Clarendon Press, Chapter 3.

Regan, D. (1980), *Utilitarianism and Co-operation*, Oxford: Clarendon Press, Chapter 5.

On the place of rules in act-utilitarianism:

Hare, R. M. (1981), *Moral Thinking*, Oxford: Clarendon Press, Part 1.

Pettit, P. and Brennan, G. (1986), 'Restrictive consequentialism', *Australian Journal of Philosophy*, Vol. 64, 438–455.

CHAPTER ELEVEN

CONCLUSIONS

We have now scrutinized utilitarianism from various angles, and it is time to weigh up the pros and cons. In doing this, I shall also remind you of the main problems with utilitarianism, the sources of each of these problems, and the best utilitarian responses.

In Chapter Three, I drew attention to some important theoretical virtues of classical utilitarianism. It is clear, simple, explanatorily powerful, and internally coherent. It also captures some attractive ideas about the marks of practical rationality and morality: it asks us to maximize the good and minimize the bad, and it is impartial – moral conflicts should be solved from an impartial standpoint where no person is singled out and given more weight than another (this standpoint need not necessarily be a detached one since it can be seen as one of generalized self-concern). Finally, it squares well with many of our intuitive moral judgements, for example, that the numbers count in life-boat cases – we ought to save the greater number of people.

I argued in Chapter Four that the subjective conception of well-being, embraced by classical utilitarians, is untenable. It is too concerned with how things feel from the inside. In particular, no weight is given to whether our pleasures and desires concern something real and valuable. In its hedonist guise, the subjective conception of well-being would have to accept that victims of illusions, such as our poor Truman, have great lives so long as they experience a lot of pleasure. In its desire-based guise, it would think highly of the lives of grass-counters, 'bare persons', dominated housewives, sadists, and vicious racists so long as their peculiar desires are satisfied. But we do not want to say that these sad characters are leading lives that are very good for them, for their lives are concerned with what is illusory or valueless. Nor do we want to say that we ought to make the world a better place by promoting lives that are concerned with the illusory or the valueless. A more plausible conception of well-being would agree with the subjective one that a life cannot be good for a person if it is not favoured by him, but will add that how good a favoured life is for a person depends crucially on how worthy of concern it is. If this hybrid conception of well-being conception is adopted by utilitarianism, the theory will now say that we ought to make the world better by promoting people's favouring of what is real and worthy of being favoured, which is a much more attractive claim. My conclusion here is therefore that we should depart from classical utilitarianism by rejecting the subjective conception of well-being in favour of a hybrid one.

The topic of Chapter Five was the aggregation of well-being. I showed that because of its commitment to sum-ranking, the particular form of welfarism accepted by classical utilitarians, utilitarianism has been unfairly accused of not caring about the well-being of individuals, not taking seriously the distinction between persons, and not treating persons as anything more than containers of well-being. These are all unfair accusations, because the utilitarianism cares about each person for her own sake and therefore cares about each person's good for its own sake. Overall well-being has intrinsic value only in virtue of being an aggregate of intrinsically valuable well-being levels of individuals. What is radical about utilitarianism is that it cares *equally* about everyone's well-being. This, in part, is what explains why utilitarianism sometimes gives counter-intuitive moral prescriptions. Among the most counter-intuitive ones are, (a) any sacrifice no matter how great can be justified if we make sufficiently many other people slightly better off, (b) inequality of well-being does not matter, and (c) a large population with people barely worth living can be better than a much smaller population of people with very happy lives. I argued that problems (a) and (b) can be dealt with at least to some extent, if we adopt a prioritarian aggregation method, according to which the lower well-being levels of worse off people are assigned more weight. If considered more thoroughly, (c) is a problem that would quickly lead us into the perplexing area of population ethics, an area that falls outside the aims of this book. Since it is not clear exactly how much weight should be given to worse off people, sum-ranking still stands out as the simpler and more straightforward method of aggregation. But in the light of its more counter-intuitive implications, I am inclined to reject it in favour of some form of prioritarianism.

In Chapter Six, I asked whether utilitarianism is a user-friendly guide to action. In particular, I focused on the question of whether we can easily know what we ought to do according to utilitarianism. My conclusion was negative. Since it is very difficult to know the future consequences of our actions, it is very difficult to know what we ought to do. Even if we reformulate the utilitarian theory in epistemic terms so that it asks us to maximize expected value (defined in terms of epistemic probabilities), the problem remains, for it is not much easier to know what maximizes expected value than what maximizes actual value. However, this negative conclusion should be put in perspective because other non-utilitarian moral theories are more or less in the same boat. These non-utilitarian theories face the knowledge problem because they trade in unclear and vague terms, lack principles about how to weigh conflicting duties, or require knowledge about hidden facts about the past or people's deep psychological make-up. In fact, if these non-utilitarian theories also accept a prima facie duty to prevent future suffering, they seem to be in a worse position to know their moral duties.

In Chapter Six, I also discussed the objection that utilitarianism is not user-friendly because it asks for unrealistic motivations in moral agents. I argued that utilitarianism does not require that agents care equally about everyone. It is true that the *theory* gives equal weight to everyone, but moral agents are only required to *do* what will bring about the impartially best outcome. They need not be exclusively concerned with the impartially best outcome in order to act rightly. Finally, I pointed out that sometimes utilitarianism condemns itself as a guide to action, but I denied that this shows that the theory is unacceptable. Once we note that a moral theory, such as utilitarianism, is first and foremost a criterion of rightness and not a decision method, it should not be surprising that it can tell you not to be motivated to act in accordance with it. I showed that this holds for non-utilitarian theories as well. For example, a virtue ethics that states that what matters fundamentally is that the agent leads a flourishing life will accuse the agent of the vice of self-indulgence, if he acts in accordance with the theory and is moved by thoughts about his own flourishing. The tentative conclusion of Chapter Six was therefore that no plausible moral theory will easily be applied by all agents in all situations.

In Chapter Seven, I turned to the question whether utilitarianism is too demanding. I noted that utilitarianism does not require us to act heroically if we lack heroic motivational capacities and are thus unable to act heroically. However, it does ask for acts of self-sacrifice in tragic situations in which overall well-being can only be promoted at the expense of the well-being of the agent. Utilitarianism asks for these actions in the sense that it claims that they are obligatory, but this does not mean that we are automatically blameworthy if we fail to do what is obligatory. For one thing, we can have a good excuse, for example, that the obligatory action asked for an enormous sacrifice.

I also pointed out that common-sense morality will ask for great sacrifices if reasonable moral demands are repeated over time. Virtue ethics, at least in some forms, will be as demanding as utilitarianism, if it says that we ought to do what a *fully* virtuous person would do. Kantianism, in its most austere form, will often be very demanding since it will tell us not to lie, cheat, or break a promise even if this is the only way we can save ourselves or our friends and family from being seriously harmed.

One reason why utilitarianism is more demanding than some non-utilitarian theories is that it is wedded to maximizing act-consequentialism. Only the action with the *best* consequences is good enough and hence obligatory. This means that there is no room for doing something morally desirable that goes beyond the call of duty. Nothing can be better than duty. However, this notion of going beyond the call of duty is problematic, since it assumes that some actions are morally better than duty, but still only optional, not obligatory. But how can we be permitted to do what is morally worse than some other available option? I suggested that one way to solve this problem would be to say that we *ought* to perform an act of heroic self-sacrifice, if it is better than all other options, but we are not always *required* to it in order to avoid blame. This solution is of course acceptable to utilitarians as well.

In the last section of the chapter I discussed in dialogue form the question whether utilitarians can be good friends. My conclusions were that, yes, they can be good friends, because they can care about others for their own sakes – the utilitarian agent who only cares about overall well-being is a caricature. However, I also pointed out that moral motivation, no matter whether it is utilitarian or non-utilitarian in nature, can be an obstacle to intimate relationships. Sometimes the morally right thing is not to think in terms of what is morally right.

In Chapter Eight, I discussed the question of whether utilitarianism is too permissive. In particular, I asked whether it is true that it must reject constraints and special duties. I argued that it is true that classical utilitarianism can at most assign instrumental value to constraints and special duties, but non-classical utilitarianism can assign intrinsic value to constraints and special duties. To be intentionally harmed or lied to, can be seen as being intrinsically bad for you. Similarly, to be cared for or saved by your own parent can be seen as being intrinsically good for you. Now, some of these claims would require a drastic revision of our normal ideas about what can be intrinsically good or bad for people. But a *non-utilitarian* consequentialist is free to say that they are intrinsically bad or good, but not intrinsically bad or good for anyone, a possibility which I think tends to speak in favour of this version of consequentialism.

No matter which form of consequentialism is adopted, there are still limits on the way constraints and special duties can be accommodated. Any consequentialist must say that we ought to violate a constraint or a special duty in order to minimize the number of similar violations, since, more generally, the bad ought to be minimized. Many deontologists would balk at this idea. But I argued that it is surprisingly difficult to find a good explanation of why we are not permitted to commit a violation in order to minimize the number of similar violations. The best explanation on offer invokes the notion of inviolability, but this notion seems to presuppose a controversial distinction between doing and allowing harm that is denied by utilitarians (and consequentialists).

This distinction and others that relate to the way outcomes are brought about was the topic of Chapter Nine. Here I used the famous Trolley problem to show what is at stake between utilitarians and non-utilitarians. I contrasted the utilitarian 'solution', that it is permissible for the doctor to cut up a healthy patient to use his organs to save five other patients, with the ones offered by the act/omission principle, double-effect doctrine and the Kantian humanity principle. I pointed out some conceptual difficulties with the distinctions underlying these principles. It is not clear how to distinguish acts from omissions, intended effects from foreseen effects, and treating a person as an end from treating him merely as a means. I also showed that none of the principles does in fact give an intuitively attractive solution to the Trolley problem. I also tried to make the utilitarian solution more attractive by pointing out that in real life any rational utilitarian doctor has to take into account the risk of people knowing about his actions and the risk that his actions will fail to save the five patients. It is therefore highly unlikely that it would be rational for a utilitarian agent to go ahead with the enforced donation in a real-life situation. I also pointed out that no sane utilitarian would urge doctors to implement such a donation policy. Furthermore, the strong aversion we feel towards this kind of killing is perfectly justifiable in terms of the bad consequences of giving up this aversion.

In Chapter Ten, finally, I turned to the question as to whether act-utilitarianism should be abandoned in favour of rule-utilitarianism. I showed that the rule-utilitarian theory does not collapse into act-utilitarianism. It is a coherent alternative form of utilitarianism, but there are some serious problems about how best to formulate the theory in light of the standard objections about partial compliance, disaster prevention, and the lack of a unique best system of rules. I also pointed out that the rule-utilitarian prescriptions will to some extent coincide with those of common-sense morality. However, this does not mean that rule-utilitarianism is closer to common-sense morality than act-utilitarianism with respect to the proposed *explanation* of what makes actions right or wrong. On the contrary, in this respect act-utilitarianism comes closer to common sense, since they agree that in many cases what matter fundamentally are the direct consequences of an action on the well-being of a person (or an animal). In these cases it is simply out of place to raise the rule-utilitarian question about what the consequences would be if everyone followed or accepted a certain kind of a rule.

The upshot of this critical discussion is that the most plausible form of utilitarianism will not be the classical one. True, it will agree with the classical version in accepting maximizing act-consequentialism, but it will reject the subjective conception of well-being in favour of a hybrid conception that incorporates both subjective and objective elements. Arguably, it should also deny sum-ranking and instead adopt a prioritarian aggregation method. The discussion of constraints and special duties shows that there is some pressure to go even further and deny welfarism and claim that some things can be good or bad and thus morally relevant without being good or bad for people. However, this is not a major departure from welfarism. First, the goods and bads relating to constraints and special duties are not completely detached from people. Even if they are not good and bad *for* people, they still *involve* people, since they concern the way people are treated. Second, any plausible consequentialist theory will give a prominent place for the well-being of people. For example, the suffering of people will be given paramount moral importance.

Of course, I do not pretend that I have conclusively argued for these controversial conclusions; I have only provided suggestive argumentative hints. But an introductory book is not the place for detailed argumentation for controversial conclusions. Much less controversial are my conclusions about the significance of the standard objections to utilitarianism. I think it is pretty clear that the utilitarian should not be too bothered by the objections that his theory is demanding and not especially user-friendly, since any plausible moral theory will have to deal with these problems. The problems that are unique to utilitarianism and thus more pressing concern its lax attitude towards constraints, special duties, and the way outcomes are brought about. It is here the utilitarian will have to admit that his theory requires a radical rethinking of many cherished elements of common-sense morality. Whether this rethinking can be justified is a question I leave for you to answer.

NOTES

CHAPTER ONE INTRODUCTION

1. Peter Singer, *Animal Liberation: A New Ethics for Our Treatment of Animals*, New York: Random House, 1975. Second edition published by Random House in 1990.
2. Jeremy Bentham, *The Principles of Morals and Legislation*, London: T. Payne, 1823, (originally printed 1789), footnote 1, p. 311.
3. John Rawls, *A Theory of Justice*, Oxford University Press, 1972.
4. Fred Feldman, *Utilitarianism, Hedonism, and Desert*, Cambridge University Press, 1997, p. 13.

CHAPTER TWO THE NATURE AND ASSESSMENT OF MORAL THEORIES

1. Of course, not all conditionals of this kind should be read this way. When I say that if you are going to shoot up heroin, you ought to use clean needles, I am not saying that your shooting up heroin makes it right to use clean needles to shoot up heroin. Rather, I am implying that shooting up heroin with clean needles is preferable to shooting up heroin with dirty needles. This is compatible with it being wrong to shoot up heroin in the first place.
2. Frank Jackson, *From Metaphysics to Ethics: A Defence of Conceptual Analysis,* Oxford: Oxford University Press, 1998, p. 135.

CHAPTER THREE WHAT IS UTILITARIANISM?

1. I have borrowed the term 'sum-ranking' from Amartya Sen. See, for instance, his and Bernard Williams' edited volume *Utilitarianism and Beyond*, Cambridge University Press, 1982, Introduction.
2. Jeremy Bentham, *The Principles of Morals and Legislation*, Oxford, 1823, (originally printed 1789), Chapter 17, Section 4, footnote 1, p. 311.
3. Ibid., Chapter 4, Section 6.
4. John Stuart Mill, *Utilitarianism*, London: Longmans, Green, Reader & Dyer, Chapter 2, Section 19.
5. Jeremy Bentham, *The Principles of Morals and Legislation*, Chapter 1, Section 2, p. 2.
6. Ibid., Chapter 1, Section 10, p. 4.

7. Henry Sidgwick, *The Methods of Ethics*, Seventh Edition, London: Macmillan and Co Ltd, 1907, (originally published 1874), Book IV, Chapter 1, Section 1, p. 411.
8. G. E. Moore, *Ethics*, Oxford University Press, 1961 (originally published 1912), Chapter 1, especially p. 37.
9. For a full story consult Richard Hare, *Moral Thinking*, Oxford: Clarendon Press, 1981, Part 2.
10. I have ignored another influential Kantian principle here, namely, that according to which an action is wrong if and only if it is forbidden by a principle that no one can reasonably reject. This so-called contractualist principle has recently been defended by T. M. Scanlon in his *What We Owe to Each Other*, Harvard University Press, 1998. The reason why I ignore this principle is that it is now mainly understood as a *metaethical* principle which provides an analysis of the property or the concept of wrongness. Scanlon himself makes this clear in ibid., footnote 21, p. 391.

CHAPTER FOUR WELL-BEING

1. William James, *The Will to Believe, Human Immortality and Other Essays on Popular Philosophy*, Mineola, NY: Dover Publications Inc., 1956, p. 32.
2. Fred Feldman, *Pleasure and the Good Life*, Oxford University Press, 2004, pp. 9–10; and Stephen Darwall, *Welfare and Rational Care*, Princeton, NJ: Princeton University Press, 2002, Chapter 1.
3. This example was first presented in Robert Nozick, *Anarchy, State, and Utopia*, New York: Basic Books, 1974, pp. 42–45.
4. Fred Feldman, *Pleasure and the Good Life*, pp. 56–57.
5. For a similar account of favouring, see Tom Hurka, *Virtue, Vice, and Value*, Oxford University Press, 2001, pp. 13–14.
6. For a similar account of disfavouring, see Ibid.
7. These principles are best seen as defining what is intrinsically good and bad for a person, in a *basic, underived* sense. For a situation can be intrinsically good or bad for a person without the situation *itself* being favoured or disfavoured by him; it is enough that he favours or disfavours some *part* of the situation. A situation that contains parts that are favoured or disfavoured by the person is intrinsically good or bad for him in a non-basic, derived sense, since it has intrinsic value for him in virtue of containing something that has intrinsic value for him in a more basic sense.
8. Wayne Sumner, *Welfare, Happiness, and Ethics*, Oxford: Clarendon Press, 1996, p. 125.
9. Ibid.
10. Amartya Sen, *On Ethics and Economics*, Blackwell, Oxford, 1987, pp. 45–46.
11. Richard Hare, *Moral Thinking*, p. 142.
12. John Rawls, 'Social unity and primary goods', in Amartya Sen, Bernard Williams, (eds.), *Utilitarianism and Beyond*, Cambridge University Press, 1990, p. 181.
13. Ibid.

14. John Stuart Mill, *Utilitarianism*, Chapter 2, Sections 5 and 6.
15. This circularity problem is stated in Wayne Sumner, *Welfare, Happiness, and Ethics*, pp. 164–165.
16. For a similar view, see Joseph Raz, *The Morality of Freedom*, Oxford: Clarendon Press, 1986, pp. 305–307, 317.

CHAPTER FIVE UTILITARIAN AGGREGATION

1. John Rawls, *A Theory of Justice*, p. 27.
2. Thomas Nagel, *The Possibility of Altruism*, Oxford University Press, 1970, p. 138.
3. John Stuart Mill, *Utilitarianism*, Chapter 5, Section 36, footnote 2.
4. Thomas Scanlon, *What We Owe to Each Other* p. 235.
5. John Broome, *Weighing Lives*, Oxford: Oxford University Press, 2004, p. 58.
6. Henry Sidgwick, *Methods of Ethics*, Book 3, Chapter 13, Section 3, p. 382.
7. Derek Parfit, *Reasons and Persons*, Oxford: Clarendon Press, 1992, Part 2, Chapter 17.
8. As Roger Crisp convincingly argues in his *Reasons and the Good*, Oxford: Oxford University Press, 2006, pp. 148–149.
9. Brad Hooker, *Ideal Code, Real World*, Oxford: Oxford University Press, 2000, p. 61.

CHAPTER SIX A USER-FRIENDLY GUIDE TO ACTION?

1. Robert Nozick, *Anarchy, State, and Utopia*, New York: Basic Books, 1974.
2. William K. Frankena, *Ethics*, second edition, Englewood Cliffs, NJ: Prentice-Hall, p. 116.
3. The example is from G. Oddie and P. Menzies, 'An objectivist guide to subjective value', *Ethics*, Vol. 102, No. 3, 1992, p. 512.
4. This argument is from Michael Zimmerman, *Living with Uncertainty. The Moral Significance of Ignorance*, Cambridge: Cambridge University Press, 2008, pp. 19–21.
5. The example is from Frank Jackson, 'Decision-theoretic consequentialism and the nearest and dearest objection', *Ethics*, Vol. 101, 1991, pp. 462–463. I have relabeled the options. An example of the same structure can be found in Donald Regan, *Utilitarianism and Co-operation*, Oxford: Clarendon Press, 1980, pp. 264–265.
6. This line of argument is pursued by Michael Zimmerman, *Living with Uncertainty. The Moral Significance of Ignorance*, p. 35.
7. John Stuart Mill, *Utilitarianism*, Chapter 2, Section 19.
8. Henry Sidgwick, *Methods of Ethics*, Book 4, Chapter 1, Section 1, p. 413.
9. Ibid., Book 2, Chapter 3, Section 2, p. 136.
10. This is pointed out by Tom Hurka, *Virtue, Vice, and Value*, Oxford University Press, 2001, pp. 246–249.

11. Peter Railton, 'Alienation, consequentialism, and the demands of morality', *Philosophy and Public Affairs*, Vol. 13, No. 2, 1984, pp. 134–171.

CHAPTER SEVEN IS UTILITARIANISM TOO DEMANDING?

1. The example is from Brad Hooker, *Ideal Code, Real World*, p. 73.
2. Michael Slote defends satisficing consequentialism in *Common-Sense Morality and Consequentialism*, London: Routledge and Kegan Paul, 1985, and *Beyond Optimizing: A Study of Rational Choice*, London: Harvard University Press, 1991.
3. The example about the tennis player is from Peter Railton, 'Alienation, consequentialism, and the demands of morality', *Philosophy and Public Affairs*, Vol. 13, No. 2, 1984, pp. 134–171.

CHAPTER EIGHT IS UTILITARIANISM TOO PERMISSIVE?

1. A version of this popular example was originally presented in W. D. Ross, *The Right and The Good*, Oxford: Clarendon Press, 1930, pp. 34–35.
2. Thomas Nagel discussed this example in *The View From Nowhere*, New York: Oxford University Press, 1986, p. 176.
3. A very popular example, made famous by H. J. McCloskey, 'An examination of restricted utilitarianism', *Philosophical Review*, Vol. 66, 1957, pp. 466–485.
4. Discussed in Judith Jarvis Thomson, 'Killing, letting die, and the Trolley problem', *The Monist*, Vol. 59, 1976, pp. 204–217.
5. Henry Sidgwick, *Methods of Ethics*, Book 4, Chapter 3, Section 3.
6. One possible problem with this form of consequentialism is that the badness of constraint violations may have to do with the *wrongness* of the violation. A consequentialist would then face the circularity problem we briefly discussed in Chapter Three in relation to a 'moralized' conception of well-being: Wrongness is determined (in part) by badness, which in turn is determined (in part) by wrongness.
7. Robert Nozick, *Anarchy, State and Utopia*, New York: Basic Books, 1974, p. 137.
8. Donald Regan, *Utilitarianism and Co-operation*, p. 208.
9. This explanation of inviolability is provided by Frances Kamm in *Intricate Ethics*, Oxford University Press, 2007, Chapter 1, Section 6, pp. 26–30.

CHAPTER NINE THE WAY OUTCOMES ARE BROUGHT ABOUT

1. The example was first presented in Philippa Foot, 'The problem of abortion and the doctrine of double effect', *Oxford Review, Vol.* 5, 1967, pp. 5–15.
2. Richard Hare, *Moral Thinking*, p. 132.
3. The example is from Judith Jarvis Thomson, 'The Trolley problem', in *Rights, Restitution, and Risk: Essays in Moral Theory*, edited by

W. A. Patent, Cambridge, MA: Harvard University Press, 1986, pp. 94–116.
4. Ibid.
5. Joshua Greene, (forthcoming), 'The Secret Joke of Kant's Soul', in *Moral Psychology,* Vol. 3: *The Neuroscience of Morality: Emotion, Disease, and Development*, edited by Sinnott-Armstrong, Cambridge, MA: MIT Press.

CHAPTER TEN THE PLACE OF RULES IN UTILITARIANISM

1. As far as I know, Donald Regan was the first to present a counterexample of this kind. See his *Utilitarianism and Co-operation*, pp. 83–93.
2. Brad Hooker, *Ideal Code, Real World*, pp. 80–85.
3. Ibid., p. 84.
4. Brad Hooker, 'Act-consequentialism versus Rule-consequentialism', *Politeia, Vol.* 24, 2008, pp. 75–85.
5. Brad Hooker, *Ideal Code, Real World*, p. 32, and ibid.
6. John Stuart Mill, *Utilitarianism*, Chapter 2, Section 23, p. 70.
7. Shaun Nichols, *Sentimental Rules*, Oxford University Press, 2004, pp. 5–6.
8. For more on their radical views see, for instance, Peter Singer, *Rethinking Life and Death. The Collapse of Our Traditional Ethics*, Oxford: Oxford University Press, 1995 and Peter Unger, *Living High and Letting Die*, Oxford: Oxford University Press, 1996.
9. Peter Singer, *Practical Ethics*, Cambridge University Press, 1979, p. 181.

INDEX